1969

This

ARGONAUT LIBRARY OF ANTIQUITIES

ALEXANDER THE GREAT
IN GREEK AND ROMAN ART

ALEXANDER THE GREAT IN GREEK AND ROMAN ART

by

Margarete Bieber

ARGONAUT, INC., PUBLISHERS
CHICAGO MCMLXIV

Library of Congress Catalogue Card Number: **LC 64-23430**

ARGONAUT INC., PUBLISHERS
737 NORTH MICHIGAN AVE.
CHICAGO, ILL. 60611

PRINTED IN THE UNITED STATES OF AMERICA

TABLE OF CONTENTS

ACKNOWLEDGMENT

My thanks are due to the American Council of Learned Societies for making a grant for photographing sculpture and making enlarged individual photographs of each coin; to the late Agnes Baldwin Brett for selecting the coins from the American Numismatic Society in New York; to the directors of the Metropolitan Museum of Art and the Boston Museum of Fine Arts, who have liberally allowed me to use their treasures. My warmest thanks are due to Dean Jacques Barzun of Columbia University who awarded me a research grant to continue my scholarly work on this book, and to the American Philosophical Society which kindly granted permission for the use of the article "The Portraits of Alexander the Great," in the *Proceedings* of the Society, Vol. 93, no. 5, 1949, pp. 373-426. I also wish to thank the editor, Mr. Al. N. Oikonomides, for his help in finding new illustrations and necessary information.

INTRODUCTION

SEVERAL monographs on the portraits of Alexander the Great have been written. They all contain some valuable material, but none of them is complete, and none has a satisfactory arrangement. The best monograph by J. J. Bernoulli, *Die erhaltenen Darstellungen Alexanders des Grossen,* München, Bruckmann, 1905, distinguishes between ethical and emotional portraits, which occur, however, in the same periods. Ch. de Ujfalvi, *Le type physique d'Alexandre le Grand, d'après les auteurs anciens et les documents iconographiques,* Paris, Fontemoing, 1902, treats in detail only of Alexander's actual appearance. Th. Schreiber, "Studien über das Bildnis Alexanders des Grossen, Ein Beitrag zur Alexandrinischen Kunstgeschichte, mit einem Anhang uber die Anfänge des Alexanderkultus" in *Abhandlungen der sächsischen Gesellschaft der Wissenschaften 21* (3), 1903, and more recently K. Gebauer, "Alexanderbildnis und Alexandertypus," in *Mitteilungen des Deutschen archäologischen Instituts 63/4:* 1-106, 1938/9, deal particularly with those posthumous statues and heads which come from Alexandria. Gebauer distinguishes original and copies. E. G. Suhr, *Sculptured Portraits of Greek Statesmen,* with a special study of Alexander the Great, *The Johns Hopkins University Studies in Archaeology,* No. *13:* 46-133, 1931, makes the turn of the head to the right or left the distinguishing characteristic.

The main fault in all these monographs is the fact that none distinguishes between the different periods in which the bewildering varieties of Alexander portraits, preserved for us, have been created. It is a parallel to the mass of writers who have dealt with Alexander in antiquity as well as in our time. "There is no one about whom more have written, and more in disagreement with each other," says Arrian in his Preface to the *Anabasis of Alexander.* Yet he continues:

> *But in my opinion the narratives of Ptolemy and Aristobulus are more worthy of credit than the rest; Aristobulus, because he served under King Alexander in his expeditions, and Ptolemy, not only because he accompanied Alexander in his expeditions, but also because being a king himself, the falsification of facts would have been more disgraceful to him than to any other man.*

This critical use of his sources has made Arrian our soundest and most trustworthy source for the life of Alexander, despite the fact that he lived in the second century A.D. under Hadrian and Antoninus Pius. Plutarch, only a little earlier, for he is said to have been the teacher of Hadrian and died about A.D. 120, used the same sources, but also others less reliable, like invented speeches and letters of Alexander. His description of the appearance of Alexander is based on the portraits made by the court sculptor Lysippos. We thus have in these Greek writers of the Roman period a parallel to the copies of contemporary portraits made mostly by Greek sculptors for the Roman masters. The original statues and paintings are mostly lost, but the copies are, like the writings of Arrian and Plutarch, so reliable that they can take their place. It is of course to be regretted that in both cases we do not have the originals. Ptolemy was the earliest and most intimate friend of Alexander, his most skillful general, who accompanied him throughout his campaigns and had access to the royal Ephemerides, the court journal of Alexander's expeditions and other official material. Aristobulus of Potidaea in Macedonia also accompanied Alexander as a technician and expert engineer, and he was interested in geography and natural history. Both works of these contemporaries, however, appeared only after Alexander's death and thus belong to the time of his successors, as many portraits do. Plutarch also used a contemporary account of Callisthenes of Olynthus, the historian who accompanied Alexander on his expeditions and who has been called his press agent. To him are due some extravagant inventions like the early deification of Alexander. But when he opposed the Persian custom of prostration to Alexander for Macedonians, and was connected with a conspiracy against Alexander, he was put to death in 327 B.C. His reports were partly used by Cleitarchus, a secondary source, as he did not accompany Alexander and as his history of Alexander was written probably in the early third century B.C. His romantic rhetorical and sometimes bombastic style is therefore parallel and contemporary to the portraits which the successors of Alexander set up. From Cleitarchus stems the Alexander Romance, which we find in the early Roman Diodorus Siculus in his *Universal History, Book XVII*, from the time of Caesar and Augustus, and in Quintus Curtius Rufus, *De gestis Alexandri Magni,* from the time of Claudius, based on Trogus Pompeius who wrote in the time of Augustus. Curtius also used other writers, particularly the "mercenaries source" based on tales of the Greek mercenaries, mostly refugees from their cities, who served in the army of Darius against Alexander. More unfavorable traits were brought from the philosophical schools, the peripatetic to which the executed Callisthenes, nephew and pupil of Aristotle, had belonged, as well as the stoic school, who conceived of Alexander as an arrogant and proud conqueror. They believed that it was Fortune alone which had led him to success, not his character. Two quite different literary character portraits are found in these sources: the perfectly virtuous pupil of Aristotle, and the later Alexander who became a cruel tyrant. Despite these exaggerations the distinction between the earlier and the later character of Alexander to me seems right in principle and a parallel to the distinction between the portraits of Alexander as a conqueror of Persia and as the Great King of Asia. Plutarch in his *De Alexandri Fortuna* has rightly protested against the distorted picture of the philosophers; he regarded Alexander as a philosopher in action. In his comparison of the Lives of Alexander and Caesar, he has shown how Alexander, despite impatience and irritability, by daring and bravery makes Fortune yield her power to his plans.[1]

We thus have in the ancient literature several portraits of Alexander which are partly contemporary, partly follow each other, and partly turn back to older pictures, but with newly invented traits. This, in my opinion, is to be expected in the art of the Alexander portraits also. It is quite clear that the young pupil of Aristotle looked different as crown prince and as commander-in-chief of the Greek army and again different when he became ruler of an enormous empire. We also know, particularly from Pliny, *Natural History,* Books XXXIV-XXXV, that different artists portrayed him at different periods. From childhood on he was portrayed by Lysippos; as a young general and crown prince he was portrayed, together with his father and mother, by Leochares. Euphranor

[1] Latest and best investigation of the literary sources: Tarn, W. W., *Alexander the Great,* II, Sources and Studies: 1-133, 286-309, Cambridge, Univ. Press, 1948, Pt. I has been reprinted by Beacon Press, Boston, 1956 and 1962. Pearson, L., *The Lost Histories of Alexander,* New York 1960.

and Chares or Chaereas also portrayed him at an unknown period, together with Philip. But while he was king he allowed himself to be portrayed from life only by Lysippos, Apelles, and Pyrgoteles. Nobody, however, could prevent the other artists from modeling, carving, or painting him, any more than he could prevent writers who were not invited to follow his expeditions, from writing about his deeds. Thus we know that Euthycrates, the pupil of Lysippos, sculptured Alexander as a hunter; Protogenes painted him with Pan; Aetion painted his wedding with the Bactrian princess Roxane. These pictures certainly belong to the period when he was on his expeditions in Persia, while paintings by Nikias and Antiphilos, who painted him as a boy, and another time with Philip and Athena, may belong to an earlier period. On the other hand Philoxenos of Eretria painted the battle of Alexander and Darius, commissioned by Krateros, certainly after the death of Alexander. An unknown artist painted the figure of the king in his chariot on his funeral carriage (Diodor, XVIII, 26). Many other portraits by unknown artists are mentioned. It is clear that the growing romance of Alexander's life must have inspired the artists still more than the facts during his lifetime. Many rulers like Demetrius of Bactria, in the second century, Mithridates and Pompey in the first century B.C., and even Caracalla in the third century A.D. tried to imitate his appearance, transmitted by portraits. The Romans were the true heirs to Alexander's Empire much more than the diadochi who only carved portions out of it for themselves. But the Romans were really the rulers of the whole empire once conquered by Alexander and divided into states by his successors. The Romans were not only the political heirs, but also inherited his new ideas about the fusion of all mankind into one harmonious world, regardless of race and religion. Caracalla in A.D. 212 admitted all free inhabitants of the whole Roman Empire to citizenship, as Alexander had planned for the Persians and other non-Greeks, who up to this time had been considered, even by his teacher Aristotle, as "barbarians." We have here ideas which have been taken over by the Christian religion and which are brought into practice in our time only in the United States. The British, French, Belgian, Dutch, Portuguese, and all Empires still distinguish between subjects and citizens.[2]

No wonder that the personality of Alexander, his generosity and exuberant nature combined with conscious pose and deliberate action, his broad outlook and his romantic beauty, have enchanted writers, poets, and artists alike. He attracted the subtlest Greek and the rudest barbarian. His army and his Macedonian friends worshipped him as a hero even while he still lived. Although occasionally rebellious, they always followed him to his battles, not one of which he lost. His successes and the tragic losses of his friends, partly through his own fault, must have added to the attraction. No wonder that at all times new monographs were, and still are written on this greatest of all Greek historical figures;[3] and no wonder that again and again new portraits of him were created. The major ancient literary sources belong to four periods: (1) contemporary: Callisthenes, Ephemerides, Mercenaries; (2) time of the successors:

[2] Tarn, *op. cit.,* 399-499. Partly repeated from Alexander the Great and the Unity of Mankind, *Proc. British Academy 19*: 123-166, 1933.

[3] Robinson, Jr., Charles Alexander, *Alexander the Great,* N. Y., Dutton, 1947. The Meeting of East and West in World Government and Brotherhood, 241-244. To his list of earlier works must be added, Droysen, J. G., *Geschichte Alexanders des Grossen,* 1883, new edition ed. H. Berve, 1931. Kaerst, Julius, in Pauly-Wissowa, *Real-Encyclopädie* I: 1412-1434, no. 10; *idem, Geschichte des Hellenismus* I², Leipzig, Teubner, 1927, and Tarn, W. W., *Alexander the Great* I, Narrative, 1948.

Aristobulus, Ptolemy I, Cleitarchus; (3) early Roman, Caesar to Claudius: Diodorus Siculus, Curtius Rufus, based on Trogus Pompeius; (4) second century A.D.: Plutarch and Arrian.

The figurative representations of Alexander, in my opinion, cover a longer space of time. They can give us a complete chronological picture of the development of the conception of Alexander from his youth to the end of antiquity. I have therefore tried to arrange all important portraits of Alexander in the following eight groups:

(1) The parents of Alexander and Alexander as crown prince, to 336 B.C. Portraits made by the sculptors used by Philip.

(2) 336-330 B.C. Alexander as conqueror of Europe and Persia. The three court artists.

(3) 330-323 B.C. Alexander the Great, King of Asia, then identified with the Persian Empire.

(4) 323-300 B.C. Alexander as conceived by the diadochi, his successors.

(5) Third century B.C. Early Hellenistic, idealizing, particularly Alexandrian conception.

(6) Second century B.C. Hellenistic, emotional, particularly Asiatic conception.

(7) First century B.C. Late Hellenistic passionate and classicizing conceptions side by side.

(8) Roman Empire. Continuation and increase of late Hellenistic conceptions.

The portrait of Alexander developed according to his life and to his personality, and later in accordance with the life story which the different periods composed out of the many different reports and also on the basis of older portraits available to them. Just as has been done for the literary periods, the different periods of art and different trends of each period have to be accounted for. The later artists interpreted the features of Alexander according to their own conception, just as the later writers added romance or scepticism to their older sources of contemporary writers. We see many contemporary portraits only through their Hellenistic adaptations or their Roman copies, just as we know Ptolemy I and Aristobulus through Arrian, and Cleitarchus through Diodorus and Curtius. Yet a critical investigation will give us a clear picture of the portraits of each period.

I. THE PARENTS OF ALEXANDER AND ALEXANDER AS CROWN PRINCE

Philip II, the founder of the Macedonian Empire and father of Alexander the Great,[4] was the third son of Amyntas III, a rather insignificant king of a small state in northern Greece. The royal family, partly of Illyrian and partly of Hellenic blood, had always aspired, however, to Greek culture. When Philip was a young man of about fifteen, he was sent as a hostage to Thebes for three years (367-364 B.C.). He was further imbued with love for the higher form of civilization he found there. From then on he strove constantly to combine the warlike virtues of his people with the Hellenic culture.

Philip succeeded his two older brothers, first as regent for his infant nephew, then in 359 B.C. as king, at the age of twenty-three. He created the first national standing army organized on a broad basis. His most important addition to the infantry was the phalanx, a body of men in sixteen rows, the six front rows armed with long pikes. He first used this army to conquer all of northern Greece, the coasts near Macedonia, and Thrace. The siege of the Athenian colony Amphipolis in 357 brought him into conflict with Athens, a city which he venerated and always tried to pacify. But he needed the gold mines of

[4] Geyer, F., in Pauly-Wissowa, *Real-Enc.* XIX: 2266-2303, no. 7. Hogarth, D. G., *Philip and Alexander of Macedon,* N. Y., Scribners, 1897. Hampl, F., *Der König der Makedonen,* Weida in Thüringen, Thomas, 1934. Momigliano, A., *Filippo il Macedone,* Florence, 1934. Pickard-Cambridge, *Cambridge Anc. Hist.* II: 200-271. *Cp.* also Robinson, David, *Excavations at Olynthos,* in *Johns Hopkins Studies in Arch. 6, 9, 11-12, 18-20, 25-26, 31-32;* passim, 1933-1941.

the neighboring Mount Pangaeus; these provided him with the necessary means for attaining his political and military aims. He issued a new coinage which rivaled that of Athens, and his strong army and centralized political and financial control gave him superiority over the ineffective and vacillating policies of democratic Athens.

He then set out to conquer the Thracian Chersonese. The orator and statesman Demosthenes saw the danger and when Philip besieged Olynthus in 349, urged his compatriots to help. But they did too little and came too late; and Olynthus fell in 348 B.C. The *Philippics* and *Olynthiacs* of Demosthenes could not prevent Philip from becoming the strongest power in Greece, and the petty quarrels between the city-states gave him an excellent chance to attain a leading position. Isocrates, the great teacher of rhetoric, had prepared the way for him by calling for military and political unity under a strong leader, and the orators Demades and Aeschines were his most effective partisans. The Sacred War in 346 gave him the opportunity of defeating the Phocians and thus penetrating into central Greece and heading the Amphictyonic Council of Delphi. The Pythian games were celebrated under his presidency.

As champion of the Apollo of Delphi and patron of all Greece he was given leadership in the second Sacred War in 338, but instead of settling the Amphictyonic quarrel he used the opportunity to make himself definitely master of all Greece. Athens had hampered him in his siege of Perinthus and Byzantium in 340-339. He fortified Elateia, which threatened Thebes as well as Athens, and this led to an alliance between these two, till then, enemy states. But Philip won the decisive battle of Chaeronea. He cruelly punished his former ally Thebes, but his veneration for Athens, the center of Greek civilization, was so great that he gave to this city a good peace. In 337 at Corinth he called a congress of all the states, which were now to have a common national ideal of harmony, peace, equality, and prosperity for all under Philip's leadership. The envoys of the states at Corinth acknowledged Philip's military command and agreed to send contingents for an expedition against Persia. Philip intended only to conquer the coasts of Persia, but his plans were carried much further by his son Alexander, for Philip did not live to see his greatest dreams come true. At the wedding of his daughter Cleopatra at Aegae he was murdered by one Pausanias, perhaps at the instigation of his alienated wife, Olympias.

Several portrait statues of Philip are mentioned in literature. After the battle of Chaeronea the Athenians[5] erected a statue of Philip in their market place in gratitude for the undeservedly mild peace terms (Pausanias, 1, 9, 4; Clemens of Alexandria, *Protrepticus,* IV, 54, 5; p. 42 Staehlin). Also after Chaeronea Philip dedicated the Philippeion at Olympia, with gold and ivory statues of himself, his father, his wife Olympias, and his son Alexander, by Leochares, were set up (Pausanias, V, 20, 10).[6] A third portrait, with one of his son, was by Chaereas (Pliny, XXXIV, 75). Another statue is mentioned in the account of the fatal marriage feast at Aegae; together with the statues of the twelve chief gods it was carried into the theater (Diodorus, XVI, 92, 2). A statue by Euphranor showed Philip and Alexander on a quadriga (Pliny, XXXIV, 78). There certainly were

[5] De Falco, V., *Demade Oratore* (2nd ed), Naples, 1954, p. 4. Oikonomides, Al. N., *Hypereidou Logoi,* Athens, 1958, p. 15 note 60.

[6] Overbeck, J., *Schriftquellen,* 251, no. 1312. Bieber, M., in Thieme-Becker, *Künstlerlexikon* XXIII: 68. Lippold, G., in Pauly-Wissowa, *Real-Enc.* XII: 1993-1997. For the Philippeum *cp.* Adler, F., *Olympia* II: 128-133. Gardiner, N., *Olympia,* 131-135, Oxford, Clarendon Press, 1925.

other statues at Pella and at Philippopolis, the city founded in 355 by Philip and named after him.

The coins minted by Philip do not show his portrait.[7] It is therefore impossible to determine the source of the only portrait of Philip that has been preserved on a medallion from Tarsus at the time of Alexander Severus, now in the Bibliothèque Nationale at Paris (fig. 1).[8] This shows the great general and statesman in a richly decorated corselet, with victories on the shoulder straps and breastplate; there is also a diadem which certainly he never wore. The hair and beard are full and curly. The forehead is furrowed, the eyes shaded, and the features are not purely Greek. It may be assumed that this conception is based on a posthumous portrait, perhaps set

[7] Gaebler, H., *Die Münzen Nordgriechenlands* III, 2: 162-168, pls. XXX-XXXI, 17. Babelon, E., *Traité des Monnaies Gr. et Rom.*, ed. J. Babelon, part II, vol. IV: 499, pl. CCCIX, figs. 10-15, 1932. Seltman, Ch., *Greek coins,* 199-203, pls. XLVI, 7-14; XLVII, 1-4. Head, Barclay V., *Historia Numorum,* 223-224, Oxford, Clarendon Press, 1911, It has been supposed that the head of Apollo on the coins has been assimilated to the king and that the horseman on the coins may represent the king with a play upon his name. A certain identification is, however, impossible.

[8] Mowat, R., in *Revue Numismatique,* ser. 4, 7: 1, pl. III, 1903. Ujfalvi, Ch. de, *Le Type physique d'Alexandre le Grand,* 145, fig. 51, Paris, Fontemoing, 1902. Hogarth, *Philip and Alexander of Macedon,* plate facing p. 1. The interpretation of this coin portrait as that of Philip was first stated by Longperier in *Revue Numismatique 13*: 313, 1868. This is doubted by Arndt, P., in *Strena Helbigiana,* 16, note 2. Arndt, P., *op. cit.,* 10-18, declares as Philip's the heads called Alcibiades in the Vatican (Arndt, P., *Porträts,* pls. 467-468) and in Munich (Arndt, P., *Porträts,* pls. 469-470; Arndt-Amelung, *E. A. ant. Skulpturen,* pls. 965-967); there is also a replica of this in Copenhagen (Arndt, P., *Porträts,* pls. 1103-1104). But the head on these coins does not agree with that of the medallion which can hardly be of anyone but Philip, accompanied as it is by medallions showing the head of his great son. *Cp.* Babelon, E., in *Amer. Jour. Num., 44*: 119-121, 1910, *idem* in *Traité des Monnaies Gr. et Rome,* part II, vol. IV; 529-531, 1932. Babelon believes that the head of Zeus on the silver drachms of Philip (see Seltman, *op. cit.,* pl. XLVI, 10-12) is used for the medallion of Tarsus. The author believes that more likely a statue and not a coin was used in this case.

up by Alexander, who transferred his diadem to his father. This posthumous statue was probably the one erected in the temple of Artemis at Ephesus (Arrian, Anabasis, I, 17, 11) and pulled down in 334, a deed punished by death by the Ephesians after the arrival of Alexander.

The mother of Alexander the Great, Olympias, was the daughter of Neoptolemus of Epirus, king of the Molossians.[9] After the death of Neoptolemus her uncle became her guardian. He took her to Samothrace to be initiated in the Mysteries, and on this occasion she met Philip of Macedon. They fell in love and were married in 357 B.C. The next year Alexander was born, and in 354 a daughter, Cleopatra. In 338/7 when Philip married another Cleopatra, the niece of the general Attalus, Alexander and his mother left the court of Pella. She remained in her homeland, Epirus, while Alexander went to Illyria and then returned to Pella. Olympias persuaded Philip to give their daughter Cleopatra in marriage to her uncle Alexander, heir to the throne of Epirus. At the wedding feast Philip was murdered by Pausanias, probably at the instigation of Olympias, who, with her daughter queen of the Molossians and her son king of Macedon, now hoped to play a leading role.

Olympias returned to Pella, killed Philip's second wife and her infant son, and was indeed a very influential mistress of the court until 331. Her son loved and respected her, though she behaved violently and obstinately and interfered in the concerns of others. The regent Antipater treated her badly during the absence of Alexander, and she therefore returned to Epirus to her daughter in 331. After the death of Antipater his successor Polyperchon called her back to Pella in 319

[9] McCurdy, Grace, *Hellenistic Queens, Johns Hopkins Studies in Arch.*, no. 14: 22-46, 1932. Strasburger, in Pauly-Wissowa, *Real-Enc.* XVIII (1): 177-182, no. 5.

and made her guardian of her grandson, the little Alexander, son of Roxane. She killed the weak king Philip Arrhidaeus, his wife Eurydice, and a hundred other noble Macedonians, including Jollas, a son of Antipater. But Polyperchon was defeated and Cassander, another son of Antipater, came home to take revenge. He besieged Olympias in Pydna in 317-6, captured her, and brought her to trial. The relatives and friends of her victims acted as her judges and executioners.

The historians describe her as arrogant, meddlesome, fierce, passionate, dramatic, and romantic (Plutarch, *Life of Alexander,* IX; Arrian, *Anabasis,* VII, 12). She was an ardent follower of the orphic and bacchic mysteries. She had snakes as pets and let them wind around the sacred staff of Dionysus. From this predilection of hers probably comes the story of the god who approached Olympias in the shape of a snake and became the divine father of Alexander. The legend is represented on late Roman Macedonian coins.[10] Olympias is seated on a throne, with her himation drawn over her head and left shoulder, feeding a snake. The bust alone, with a similar arrangement of the drapery and only the right arm shown, appears on a golden medallion found at Abukir in Egypt (fig. 2),[11] on late contorniates of Macedonia

[10] Gaebler, H., *Die antiken Münzen Nordgriechenlands* III, 1: nos. 347a, 416, 527, 529, 550-551, 634-636, 721a, pl. IV, 26-27. III, 2: nos. 35, 46, pl. V, 4-5. On other coins she is lying on a couch and greeting the snake. Gaebler, H., *op. cit.,* III, 1: no. 367, pl. IV, 35; III, 2: 13, no. 34, pl. V, 3. On contorniates with a similar representation there is the inscription "Olympias regina." *Cp.* Gaebler, H., in *Ztschr. für Numismatik* 25: 13, 1906.

[11] Dressel, H.,*Fünf Goldmedaillons von Abukir,* in *Abh. preuss. Akad. d. Wiss.* 10 and 31-40, pls. II, C, and IV, 7, 1906. Koester, E., Gold Medallions of Abukir, in *Burlington Mag. 11*: 163, fig. 2, 1907. The authenticity of these medallions has been questioned, but there has not been proof of forgery. *Cp.* below, note 87.

of the time of Alexander Severus,[12] and on contorniates in Paris, Milan, and Berlin. [13] Olympias is represented with a diadem and scepter. The hair is carefully waved along her forehead. The profile is noble and regular. Around her right arm a living snake, not a stiff snake bracelet, is wound. The style is that of the second half of the fourth century.

There was a statue of Olympias at Olympia with those of Philip, his parents Amyntas and Eurydice, and Alexander, by Leochares, erected after the battle of Chaeroneia in 338 B. C. The portraits on the coins and medallions may well derive from this statue of the great queen, and she may well have been portrayed with her favorite animal. The passionate nature and romantic beauty of the remarkable woman are not expressed in these late minor works of art, but they may be found as her legacy in the portraits of her son Alexander.

It has been thought that Olympias is represented with Alexander on the large cameos in Vienna and Leningrad (figs. 3-4).[14] This is possible, although the features are those of a younger woman and the identity of Alexander is not quite certain. The serpent on his helmet, however, may allude not only to his divine descent, but also to the serpent which is said to have guided him through the desert to the oasis of Ammon.

[12] Sallet, A., *Ztschr. für Numismatik* 25: 13, and 37-38, 1906. Ujfalvy, Ch. de, *Le Type physique d'Alexandre le Grand,* 87, fig. 26. Schreiber, Th., *Studien über das Bildnis Alexanders des Grossen,* 185, fig. 22. Gaebler, H., *op. cit.,* III, 1: no. 880. Probably not a coin but a piece of jewelry or an amulet. On the reverse side is a snake.

[13] Dressel, H., *op. cit.,* pls. III, 1 and IV, 1 and 8. On the contorniate at Paris, Dressel, H., *op. cit.,* pl. IV, 1, Olympias is represented as Omphale with a lion skin instead of the himation.

[14] Furtwängler, A., *Gemmen,* pl. 53. Bernoulli, J. J., *Darstellungen Alex.,* 126-131, pls. VIII, 1, and IX, 1. Delbrück, R., *Porträts,* pl. 58, fig. 15. Eichler-Kries, *Die Kameen,* pl. I.

From his father, Philip, Alexander inherited his military virtues; from his mother, Olympias, he received his fiery and passionate nature, his ambition, his good looks, and romantic personality. Philip not only trained him in arms, but in 342 B.C., when Alexander was fourteen years old, his father gave him as teacher the most learned Greek of his time, Aristotle. Through Aristotle, the young Alexander was introduced to the culture, political life, and political theories of the Greeks, and intellectual force was thus developed in an excellent body. Aristotle made for Alexander a recension of the *Iliad.* Homer became his ideal and Achilles his hero to be emulated. He did not, however, accept all the teachings of Aristotle; the theory, for example, that all non-Greeks are barbarians and born only to be slaves was later refuted by him, both in principle and in practice, when he treated the subjected Persians as the equals of his Macedonians. He loved hunting, and is said as a boy to have tamed the wild horse Bucephalus after his father Philip had failed to do so. The taming is depicted in a bronze statuette, of probably Hellenistic-Etruscan workmanship, in the Archeological Museum at Florence (fig. 24). [14a] When only eighteen years of age Alexander fought as a general in the Battle of Chaeronea. In the quarrel of Olympias with Philip, it is interesting to note, he took his mother's side.

It is natural that the portraits of the young crown prince Alexander (340-336) were made by the artists used by his father Philip: Chaereas, Euphranor, and Leochares. Lysippos also is said to have made portraits of Alexander the Great, beginning from his boyhood

[14a] L. A. Milani, *Il Museo archeologico di Firenze* II (1912) 8, pl. XXXV, 1. Here described as an Etruscan bronze statuette representing Castor. Milani dates in the IV century B.C. Mercer, Charles, *Alexander the Great,* a Horizon Caravel Book, New York, 1962, p. 150.

(Plin. XXXIV, 63). The earliest of the known portraits of the young Alexander is the prototype of the head of which three copies are now in existence, one in Athens (fig. 5), one in Erbach Castle in Germany, and one from Madytos in Berlin.[15] They show a youth fifteen to sixteen years old, which would indicate that the original was made about 340 B.C., when Alexander was a pupil of Aristotle. In this portrait he appears gentle, serious, and graceful. The curly hair stands up rather high on his head, while some strands hang down over the forehead and temples. The head has been attributed to Lysippos and to Leochares, but in style it differs from the work of either. It is closer to the latter, but does not correspond so closely as does the Alexander Rondanini (figs. 6-8), which has been rightly attributed to Leochares on account of its resemblance to the Ganymed and the Apollo of Belvedere.[16].

This Rondanini statue shows Alexander at about the age of eighteen, thus around 338, after the battle of Chaeronea, in which he distinguished himself as a young general. The cuirass behind him shows that he was a general. His left foot is on a shield. He may have held two spears and the hands may have been clasped loosely around the knee of the right leg, which, like the arms, is

[15] Stark, K. B., *Zwei Alexanderköpfe,* pls. 1-2, 1879. Arndt, P., *Porträts,* pls. 473-476, 927-928. Bernoulli, J. J., *op. cit.,* 39-42, fig. 9, pls. II-III. Hekler, A., *Die Bildniskunst der Griechen und Römer,* pl. 63, Stuttgart, Hoffmann, 1912. Gebauer, K., *Athenische Mitteilungen 63/64*: 70-71, 1938/1939. Blümel, K., *Katalog der Sammlung antiker Sculpturen Berlin* V: 7, K203, pl. 17, 1938.

[16] Furtwängler, A., *Beschreibung der Glyptothek,* no. 298. Brunn-Bruckmann, *Denkmäler griech, und römischer Skulptur,* pl. 105. Arndt, P., *op. cit.,* pls. 183-185. Hekler, A., *Bildniskunst,* pl. 61. Ujfalvi, Ch. de, *op. cit.,* pls. X-XI. Bernoulli, J. J., *op. cit.,* 44-51, fig. 10, pl. V. Gebauer, K., *op. cit.,* 72-73. Suhr, E. G., *Sculptured Portraits of Greek Statesmen,* 105-107, fig. 17. Laurenzi, L., *Ritratti Greci,* 105, pl. XV, no. 40. *Cp.* Bieber, M., in Thieme-Becker, *Künstlerlexikon,* XXIII: 68. Restored: piece in upper right part of head, both arms, right leg.

a bad restoration by Thorwaldsen. The body is unclothed like that of a hero, but the form is individualized. The chest is strong and broad, the limbs are heavy, the neck is carefully and richly modelled. The head shows marvelous energy coupled with a tinge of the romantic. The heavy hair is much more curly than in the other youthful portraits, a device probably used as an easy means of idealization. It rises in the front like a lion's mane, which was a characteristic peculiar to Alexander, as Aelian tells us (*Varia Historia,* XII, 14), while thick curls fall in the back and at the sides onto the neck. The lower part of the brow projects, the deep-set eyes are large and animated as he gazes into the distance. The nose is slightly bent and the mouth has a strongly marked individuality.

Evelyn Harrison has rightly recognized another youthful portrait of Alexander, possibly one made by Leochares, in an unfinished bust of the so called 'Eubuleus' found in the Agora of Athens (fig. 9-10).[17] She enumerates ten replicas, most of which were executed in the Hadrianic and Antonine periods when Alexander was again highly regarded.

The romantic and higly idealized conception of the Rondanini statue is so nearly related in style to that of the Apollo of Belvedere, rightly attributed to Leochares, that it must be a work of this master. It could not, however, be a copy of the statue of Alexander set up, together with those of his parents and grandparents, on a semicircular base in the Philippeion at Olympia. These statues were of gold and ivory, therefore probably not naked but clothed and in an attitude of repose (Pausanias, V, 20, 9-10). The group showing Alexander hunting lions in Delphi was a work of a later period done by Leochares

[17] Agora S2089. Harrison, E. B., in *Hesperia,* 19 (1960), pp. 382-389, Pl. 85c, d. List of replicas on p. 382f., note 57a.

in collaboration with Lysippos (Plutarch, *Alexander* 40, 4). But Leochares undoubtedly produced other portraits of the youthful Alexander, perhaps for Athens or for Corinth. His conception was continued in some Hellenistic portraits, such as the head Guimet (fig. 11),[18] and on some coins of Lysimachus (fig. 44).

A fourth youthful portrait of Alexander has Lysippean characteristics. The best copy of this is from the Dressel collection in Dresden (fig. 12), while a similar but later head (fig. 56), is in Copenhagen.[19] The age here is about the same as in the Munich statue. The main difference between this and the other portraits is that the thick hair, though similarly arranged, is straight, probably a realistic trait. The features in their careful modeling and somewhat nervous movement bear a close relation to the Apoxyomenos by Lysippos. The head is turned to the right, a characteristic pose of Alexander. It is undoubtedly by the same sculptor who made the original of the Azara herm (figs. 13-17). The head in Geneva (figs. 26-27) is a Hellenistic work closely resembling the Azara herm and perhaps derived from the same original.[19a] The straight hair is found also on the Alexander mosaic (fig.28), the Neison gem (fig. 25), and the coins issued later by Ptolemy I and Lysimachus (figs. 40-44).

Thus these early portraits, though not directly authenticated by inscriptions, have so many affinities with

[18] Arndt, P., *op. cit.*, pls. 922-923. Gebauer, K., *op. cit.*, 44, K 22.

[19] Bernoulli, J. J., *op. cit.*, 42, pl. IV. Gebauer, K., *op. cit.*, 63, K 59, pl. 15. Suhr, E . G., *op. cit.*, 102-103, *figs.* 15-16. Hekler, A., *Bildniskunst*, pl. 60. For the portrait in Copenhagen see Poulsen, F., *Cat. Ny Carlsberg Glyptotek*, 313, no. 441, 1951. Arndt, *op, cit.*, pls. 471-472. L'Orange, H. P., *Apotheosis in ancient Portraiture*, 13-14, fig. 1. Oslo and Cambridge, Harvard Univ. Press, 1947. Poulsen, V., *Les Portraits Grecs*. Publication de la Glyptothèque Ny Carlsberg, Copenhagen 1954, 58-59, Pl. XXIII; No. 31.

[19a] Franklin P. Johnson, *Lysippos*, p. 214, frontispiece, pl. 45.

authentic likenesses that they give us a definite conception of the appearance of the crown prince Alexander. They give a picture of the unique qualities of the boy who combined the military virtues of his father with the romantic personality of his mother, and whose intellect was developed by Aristotle.

II. ALEXANDER THE CONQUEROR OF EUROPE AND PERSIA (336-330)

When in 336 B.C., at the age of twenty, Alexander succeeded his father, he inherited a Macedonia that reached from the Balkan Mountains to the coast of the Aegean Sea, and included Thessaly; the rest of Greece, moreover, was dependent on Macedonia. He also inherited not only an army of about 60,000 men, but the League of Corinth, which had to be consolidated, and the grandiose plan of Philip to lead a Panhellenic war of revenge against Persia and to free the Greeks of Asia Minor. He first hurried through Thessaly to Greece, pacified Thebes and also Athens, which like his father he treated leniently, and had himself elected general of the League in place of Philip. In 335 he went north to the Danube, defeated the Illyrians and the Triballi and made an alliance with the Celts of the upper Danube to protect the Danube against the Getae, thus securing the northern frontier of his Empire. A report that he was dead fostered an uprising in Thebes and Athens. Thebes was destroyed—only the house of Pindar was spared—but Athens was again forgiven; Alexander desired to leave behind him a contented Athens when he went to conquer Asia.

In 334, as commander-in-chief of the Corinthian League, he crossed the Dardanelles with an army of 35,000—40,000 men. Antipater, the old general and friend of Philip, was left behind as governor in Macedonia and supervisor of the Greeks; Parmenio, another friend of Philip, was made second in command in Asia.

While Parmenio fought against the Persian satraps of the coastlands and against the Greek mercenaries under Memnon, the Rhodian general of Darius, Alexander went to Ilium as a new Achilles and offered sacrifices in the old temple of Athena. On this expedition he was accompanied by philosophers like Callisthenes of Olynthus, the nephew and pupil of Aristotle, and by historians, geographers, botanists, and other scientists; later he was joined also by poets, artists, and actors.

In a wild and dangerous attack he won his first great cavalry battle on the river Granicus. As a result of this victory Alexander conquered in a short time all the Greek cities of Asia Minor, including Miletus and Ephesus, though with some of them he had trouble. They did not share his romantic enthusiasm for the free democratic government which he tried to institute everywhere, and the great warrior had to become an organizer as well. Ada, the sister of Mausolus, the satrap who died in 354, welcomed him in Caria and aided him against Memnon, who commanded Halicarnassus but fled to his fleet and died during the siege of Mytilene on Lesbos. After capturing Halicarnassus Alexander appointed Ada to act as Viceroy of Caria (Arrian, I, 23, 8). In 333 Alexander conquered all the coastal districts, as well as Lycia, Pamphylia, and Cilicia. In Tarsus he became ill but was cured by his physician Philippus. A letter from Parmenio had warned him that the physician wanted to poison him, but the generous and trusting nature of Alexander prompted him to drink the medicine given him by Philippus; and he recovered.

The decisive victory over Darius in the battle of Issus in 333 B.C. secured for Alexander the possession of all Asia Minor. The seizure of the treasure of the Persian king in Damascus put an end to the financial difficulties of Alexander. Leaving in Alexander's possession his chariot, his tent and his family, Darius fled toward the east. Alexander did not follow immediately, but went south along the coast. He besieged Tyre, the largest commercial seaport, and after seven months took the city in 332. Darius begged for surrender of his family, asked for peace and alliance, and even offered all his lands west of the river Euphrates, but Alexander proudly refused because he had already conquered that western part of the Persian empire. He now wanted all Persia, which was supposed to be all civilized Asia. In 332 he proceeded into Egypt, where he found little resistance, for Persian rule was hated there. He founded Alexandria on a well chosen site and destined to take over the commerce formerly handled by Tyre; as a result of Alexander's foresight it became the commercial center of the Levant, and has so remained to this day. While in Egypt, Alexander was crowned Pharaoh at Memphis and when he visited the sanctuary of Zeus Ammon in the oasis of Siwah he was hailed by the priests, after the Egyptian fashion, as the son of Ammon-Re.

In 331 he returned to Asia and conquered the northern and the eastern provinces of the Persian Empire. The last battle between Darius and Alexander was fought at Arbela and Gaugamela, in Mesopotamia, near the Tigris and the ruins of Nineveh. Alexander attacked and won again under great personal danger. Darius again fled, this time to Media. Babylonia was the prize of the victory. Alexander now considered himself the Great King of Persia, and for the first time named a Persian, Mazaeus (Mazaios), as satrap of Babylon. He went to Susa, where he again found rich treasures, and then to Persepolis, the capital of Persia, which he destroyed in revenge for the destruction of Greek sanctuaries in the first Persian war a century and a half before. Here he again set up a Persian as satrap of Persia. He followed Darius to

Ecbatana in 330, but before he could reach him Darius had been murdered by Bessus. Alexander sent the body to Darius' mother at Persepolis to be buried.

When Alexander became king he is said to have chosen the best artists of his time to portray him: Lysippos the sculptor, Apelles the painter, and Pyrgoteles the gem cutter. It is fortunate that the only inscribed herm of Alexander, found by the Spanish ambassador Azara in Tivoli, and now in the Louvre (figs. 13-17),[20] has a decidedly Lysippean character, which can be discerned despite the bad state of the surface.[21] The proportions agree with the head of the Apoxyomenos, though the subtleties of the movement of the muscles are lost in the superficial copy and its badly corroded surface.

The descriptions of the appearance of Alexander by Plutarch are admittedly based on the portraits of Lysippos:

> *The outward appearance of Alexander is best represented by the statues of him which Lysippos made, and it was by this artist alone that Alexander himself thought fit that he should be modelled. For those peculiarities which many of his successors and friends afterwards tried to imitate, namely, the poise of the neck, which was bent slightly to the left (in contrast to the turn of the head to the right), and the*

[20] Louvre, *Cat. Sommaire,* no. 436. Bernoulli, J. J., *op. cit.,* 21-27, fig. 1, pl. I. Hekler, A., *Bildniskunst,* pl. 62 b. Arndt, P., *op. cit.,* pls. 181-182. Ujfalvy, Ch. de, *op. cit.,* pls. II, VIII, IX. Schreiber, Th., *op. cit.,* 17-40, figs. 4-5 (Inscription), pl. 1, Al. Suhr, E. G., *op. cit.,* 85-88, fig. 10. Laurenzi, L., *op. cit.,* 103-104, pl. XIV, no. 38. Mercer, *Alexander the Great,* fig. on p. 138. Restored: hair over left eye, part of eyebrows, nose, lips, part of herm. Surface much corroded.

[21] Johnson, F. P., *Lysippus,* 213-220, pls. 43-44; 298-309, nos. 52-74, 1927, valuable texts and translations of the references to Lysippos' statues of Alexander in ancient literature.

melting glance of his eyes, this artist has accurately observed (Alexander, 4, 1, p. 666b).

For which Alexander gave to Lysippos the sole patent for making all his statues; because he alone expressed in bronze his character (ethos), and in his lineaments represented the lustre of his virtues; while others, who strove to imitate the turning of his neck and the liquid softness and brightness of his eyes were unable to preserve the manliness and lionlike fierceness of his countenance (De Alexandri Magni Fortuna aut Virtute, On the Fortune or Virtue of Alexander, II 2).

The turn of the neck and the hair standing up over the forehead like a lion's mane (anastole) are distinctly recognizable in the Azara herm, which is authenticated by the inscription (fig. 14), of the shaft:
Alexander, son of Philip of Macedon.

Ἀλέξανδρος ¦ Φιλίππου ¦ Μακε[δών].

There is a noticeable difference in the two sides of the face, and a certain Lysippean nervous play in the muscles and the hair are still recognizable, in spite of the fact that the herm is in a bad state of preservation. We must imagine the original as being much more delicately modelled, so as to bring out the small individual traits more accurately and with more feeling, and to express not only the character but also the mood of the great conqueror.

There can be no doubt that the head of this herm is a Roman copy of that of the most celebrated statue by Lysippos, the Alexander with the spear, of which Plutarch says (*De Alex. Magn. Fort. aut Virt.* II, 2, 335 B):

When Lysippos had finished the first statue of Alexander looking up with his face to the sky (as Alexander was wont to look, with his neck slightly bent) he not improperly added to the pedestal the following lines:

The statue seems to look to Zeus and say,
Take thou Olympus; me let earth obey!

A poem, *Anthologia Graeca Pal. XVI* (Plan. App. IV), no. 120, expresses a similar idea:

Lysippos modelled Alexander's daring and his whole form. How great is the power of this bronze! The King seems to be gazing at Zeus and about to say: I set Earth under my feet; thyself, Zeus, possess Olympus.

Fortunately there is a bronze statuette that agrees with this description and has the same long-shaped head and meager features as the Azara herm. It is the statuette in the Louvre, found in lower Egypt (fig 18).[22] The head is turned sharply to his right, the left of the spectator; the neck is stretched and at the same time bent to his left, exactly as described in the literary evidence. The left arm is stretched out horizontally and probably held the spear, while the right hand points to the earth which Alexander had subdued by means of his spear, as expressed in the epigram. The statuette reflects the life and free movement characteristic of the works of Lysippos, and it is easy to imagine the lively impression of motion in the famous original statue from which it was taken.

[22] Identified by Winter, F., in *Arch. Anz., 10*: 162, 1895. Johnson, F. P., *op. cit.*, 216-217, pl. 47. Bernoulli, J. J., *op. cit.*, 102-103, fig. 31. Gebauer, K., *op. cit.*, 65-66, K 61. Ujfalvy, C. de, *op. cit.*, 65, fig. 22. Schreiber, Th., *op. cit.*, 100-110, pl. VI, L. *Cp.* Bieber, M., in Thieme-Becker, *op. cit.*, XXIII: 498-499, s.v. Lysippos.

This statuette is an early Hellenistic adaptation or reflection of the original, and the fact that it was found in Egypt points to the possibility that Lysippos has created the original for the city of Alexandria, founded by Alexander in 332. It has nothing of that tendency toward deification which began with Alexander's adoption by Zeus Ammon, and the literary evidence plainly indicates that Lysippos in the original was contrasting Alexander with Zeus, representing him as the conqueror proud of his own manly, not divine powers. The date of the original, therefore, must be before the year 330. This has been denied, however, on the ground that in the Azara herm Alexander appears to be about thirty years old, which would date the statue in 326 B.C. and that in this late period Lysippos could not have seen Alexander because he was then in India. But there is no reason why Lysippos should not have followed him to the East as other artists did. According to Plutarch (*Alexander*, 72, 1, p. 704E), many artists were summoned from Greece to Ecbatana. Probably Alexander's court sculptor was among them or had preceded them, and the statue of the great conqueror may well have been commissioned for the newly-founded city of Alexandria. As to Alexander's age, active military leaders age more quickly than ordinary men and he may well have been only twenty-five when the statue was made. Furthermore, he does not appear younger in the mosaic (fig. 28) which represents him in the battle of Issos, 333 B.C., and therefore only twenty-three years old.

Another statue by Lysippos showed him still younger. Alexander was only twenty-two years old when he won his first decisive battle on the river Granicus in 334. He himself impetuously rushed across the river into the violent cavalry engagement and was in the greatest danger, when Spithridates, the satrap of Lydia and Ionia, attacked him from the rear. His life was saved on this occasion by Clitus, but twenty-five of his companions (hetairoi) fell in this battle. Alexander commissioned Lysippos to make their statues (Arrian, *Anabasis,* I, 16, 4) and to place a figure of himself among them (Velleius Paterculus, *Historia Romana* I, 11, 3-4). This group was set up in Dion in Macedonia, but in 146 B.C. Metellus Macedonicus removed it to Rome. An adaptation of the figure of Alexander from this group made after this date, thus in the late Hellenistic or Roman republican period, is the statuette found in Herculaneum, and now in Naples (figs. 19-21).[23] The rudder under the horse alludes to the river, which Alexander crossed on horseback. The style of both horse and rider is that of Lysippos. The scarf of a general over his corselet shows that the figure represents Alexander. The broad fillet without hanging ends, however, is not the diadem, for Alexander did not adopt it till 330 B.C., that is, after the death of Darius, whose successor he claimed to be. The features of the face are youthful, the hair is only slightly curled, almost as straight as in the head in Dresden (fig. 12) and in the Azara herm (figs. 13-17), but it is more disheveled; on the forehead the locks are irregular and in the back they flutter to the sway of the lively movement.

Two decadrachms in the British Museum represent Alexander riding on the rearing Bucephalus fighting Poros, who is riding on an elephant (fig. 22).[23a] The re-

[23] Arndt, P., *op. cit.,* pls. 479-480. Bernoulli, J. J., *op. cit.,* 98-101, figs. 29-30. Ujfalvy, Ch. de, *op. cit.,* pl. XVII. Johnson, F. P., *op. cit.,* 225-226, pl. 48. Gebauer, A. K., *op. cit.,* 65-66, K 62. Markman, S. D., *The Horse in Greek Art, Johns Hopkins Studies in Arch.,* no. 35: 102-103, fig. 60, 1943. Mercer, *Alexander the Great,* fig. on p. 46f.

[23a] Ch. Seltman, *Greek Coins*^{2} (1955), p. 213f., pl. 49, figs. 6-7. W. B. Kaiser, *Jahrbuch des deutschen archäologischen* Instituts 77 (1962) pp. 227ff., figs. 3-4. Mercer, *Alexander the Great,* p. 132. Another decadrachm with Alexander and Poros is in the Museum of the Numismatic Society in New York.

verse shows Alexander standing in the same Greek attire wearing cuirass and chlamys as in the statuette of figs. 19-21.

A bronze statuette of a youthful rider found in the excavations of Begram in Afghanistan, now in the Musée Guimet in Paris (fig. 23),[24] may be an echo of another famous original created by the sculptor Lysippos. The features of the face have exact parallels in known portraits of the Lysippean group. He wears Greek defensive armour and Macedonian leather greaves. The scarf of a general covers his cuirass. The hair is straight and shows the anastole, like the other portraits of Alexander belonging to the Lysippean group.

Thus Lysippos conceived of Alexander as the great military genius and statesman of exceptional but human gifts. The epigram on the Alexander with the spear points to his conviction that he was a conqueror in his own rights as a man, not a god. Plutarch (*De Iside et Osiride* 24, p. 360D) contrasts Lysippos with the second court artist, Apelles: "Lysippos the sculptor blamed the painter Apelles for drawing Alexander's picture with a thunderbolt in his hand. He himself had represented Alexander holding a spear, which was natural and proper for him as a weapon, the glory of which time would not rob him." This painting with the thunderbolt was created by Apelles for the temple of Artemis in Ephesus, and it is said that the finger of the hand seemed to project and the thunderbolt looked as though it were outside the surface of the picture (Pliny 35, 92). This perspective treatment of the hand and thunderbolt appears on the

[24] Kurz, O., *Nouvelles recherches archéologiques à Begram,* pp. 148, 287, Figs. 335-337; Oikonomides, Al. N. in *Athene,* XXII (1961), pp. 25-27, Fig. 2.

gem cut from a carnelian, now in Leningrad (fig. 25),[25] with a later inscription added by the owner Neison. This engraved gem may, therefore, be an early Hellenistic adaptation of the picture, though the addition of the aegis dates the figure not before 330, though the lean features and the eagle points to a later period, after Alexander had been apotheosized (see below). The diadem also and smooth hair agree with the earlier portraits. Apelles was probably the first artist to give Alexander the attributes of a god, a usage which later became general.

We have no means of deciding, however, whether the Neison gem and the many other Hellenistic gems with the portraits of Alexander[26] were not influenced rather by the work of the third court artist, the gem cutter Pyrgoteles, whose likenesses of Alexander are considered by ancient authorities equally as excellent and famous as those of Lysippos and Apelles (Pliny, VII, 125. Apuleius, *Florida* VII):

> *Alexander was presented with singular excellence in all his likenesses; so that in all statues, pictures and engraved gems he appears with the same vigorous aspect of a most intrepid warrior, the same genius of a mighty hero, the same beauty and freshness of youth, the same noble expansion of forehead.*

It may well be that the deification of Alexander had already been expressed by Apelles and Pyrgoteles, before this conception became general.

[25] Furtwängler, A., *Die antiken Gemmen* I: pl. 32, no. 11; II: 157-58. Schreiber, Th., *op. cit.*, 205-207, fig. 25. Bernoulli, J. J., *op. cit.*, 133-134, pl. VIII, 3. Gebauer, K., *op. cit.*, 27, G. 31. Neuffer, E., *Das Kostüm Alexanders des Grossen,* 15, N 38. *Cp. ibid.*, other representations of Alexander as Zeus. On Alexander assimilated to several divinities see Tondriau, J., in *Revue de Philologie, de Littérature et d'Histoire anciennes,* 3rd sér., 23: 41-52, 1949.

[26] Furtwängler, A., *Die antiken Gemmen,* I: pl. 31, nos. 16-17, 19-20; pl. 32, nos. 1-9; pl. 37, no. 23; II: 153, 157, 178. Gebauer, K., *op. cit.*, 25-32, G 1-58, pl. 4.

III. THE GREAT KING OF ASIA (330-323 B.C.)

The Macedonians in 330 B.C. believed the expedition of Alexander to be at an end. But the conqueror had no intention of leaving his new empire. Though he was still king of the people of Macedonia and leader of the Greek nation, he found the Oriental conception of monarchy much more congenial to his nature. He felt himself Lord of Asia and he now aspired to conquer the whole eastern world, which then was identified with Persia. Here began the last and most romantic, but tragic, part of his life.[27]

He started his campaign with the subjugation of the provinces to the south of the Caspian Sea; then he turned toward the northeast, to Bactria and Sogdiana, and reached the river Oxus. More and more he assumed the character of an Asiatic despot, even adopting the royal Persian dress.[28] This behavior led to quarrels with his Macedonians. The army became restless; his old friends were dissatisfied and could no longer understand him. Old Parmenio, already a general of Philip's and now Alexander's second-in-command, fell out of favor and his son Philotas, becoming involved in a plot against Alexander, was tried for treason and executed. Parmenio himself was killed on Alexander's order.

After having reorganized the army, Alexander crossed the Hindu Kush mountain range farther east into

[27] Bevan, E. R., in *The Cambridge History of India,* ed. E. J. Rapson, I: 345-386, 1922. Tarn, W. W., *Alexander the Great,* I: 82-120. Robinson, Ch. A., *Alexander the Great,* 169-212. All are based for the most part on Arrian, IV 22-VI 28.

[28] Neuffer, E. *Das Kostüm Alexanders des Grossen,* 10-11, 30-38, Giessen, 1929.

Turkestan, where he founded cities and appointed Persian satraps. He returned to Bactria, executed the rebel satrap Bessus, the murderer of Darius, and received reinforcements from Europe in 328. Again he crossed the Oxus and found near the river a spring of petroleum, which he was the first European to discover. He considered this a divine miracle and offered sacrifices to the unknown god that had bestowed it. He and Craterus, one of his generals, engaged in heavy fighting with Spitamenes of Sogdiana. Later another of Alexander's generals, Seleucus, married this prince's daughter, Apama, and founded the Seleucid dynasty.

In the summer of 328 Alexander had a quarrel with another Macedonian, Clitus, when both were drunk, and killed him in anger, despite the fact the Clitus had saved his life in the battle at the Granicus. Alexander repented bitterly, but the philosopher Anaxarchus assured him that kings could do no wrong. This among other things contributed to Alexander's haughtiness and pride and encouraged him, when in Bactria in 327, to try to adopt for his court the oriental custom of prostration before the royal presence. This most of his Macedonians resented, for although it was only the usual ceremony for Persians, when approaching the Great King, the Greeks interpreted it as worship. Anaxarchus, indeed, suggested that Alexander as descendant of Herakles should be gratified with divine honors, for there was no doubt that after his death he would be honored as a god. But Callisthenes of Olynthus, the nephew and pupil of Aristotle, who had earlier declared that Alexander was the son of Zeus, unexpectedly opposed. He said that Alexander was deserving of receiving the highest honors for humans, but not those reserved for gods. This is the same conception which Lysippos had, which, however, did not agree any more with the exalted position and mood of the Lord of Asia who received prostration from the most honorable Persians. Callisthenes, as a consequence, fell out of favor and, when involved in a conspiracy of Alexander's pages, died in prison (Arrian, *Anabasis* IV, 10-12).

In 327 Alexander captured the powerful Bactrian baron Oxartes and married his daughter Roxane, in order to reconcile the great eastern barons and end the costly war in eastern Iran. At the capital Bactra he ordered that native youth should be taught the Greek language and trained for his army. This army numbered now about 120,000 men.

He now set out to conquer the remaining portion of the Persian empire, India. His plans and ideas constantly grew with time and success of his expeditions. Only by and by the vastness of India was revealed to him and his scope of conquest and exploration became vaster and vaster. He first undertook to conquer the Punjab or land of the five rivers. It was ruled by several powerful rajahs. Alexander made an alliance with Taxiles, the rajah of Taxila, whose capital was a center of the Brahman religion and of commerce. Taxiles accompanied the army to fight against Porus, his personal enemy. The battle on the Hydaspes (Jhelum) River was a bloody one on account of the elephants used by Poros (fig. 22). Alexander treated the defeated and captured enemy like a king. His land as well as that of Taxiles became allied kingdoms. Alexander founded two cities on the river Hydaspes: Nicaea, victory town, and Bucephala, named after his horse (see figs. 19-24), which had died there.

While he was in India Alexander became more and more imbued with romantic ideas. When, for example, he found a site in which ivy was growing, near a city called Nysa, he thought it to be the sacred mountain of Dionysus. From now on he considered Dionysus a forerunner to his own visit to India. The sacred shield which he had taken from the temple of Troy was always carried before him in battles.

When he had reached the river Hyphasis (Beas) and when the army gazed across the plains extending to the far-away Ganges, which Alexander planned to reach, the soldiers revolted. They had been eight years in the field and now wished to end their labors and dangers and go home to their native land, not farther into unknown countries. Thus Alexander had to abandon the plan to find the eastern end of India, which he believed near. But he did stick to his resolve to sail down the Hydaspes and through the Indus River to the ocean, which he was convinced surrounded the earth. Before embarking in 326 on the Hydaspes Alexander standing on the prow of his ship offered sacrifices to his "ancestor" Herakles, to his "father" Ammon, to the gods of the Indian rivers and of the sea, and other gods. He then started down the river to the sea. Nearchos was admiral of the fleet, the army marched on both sides of the river. On his way he conquered several Indian cities. In the city of the Mallians, an independent tribe of Indians, he was in great personal danger. He went up the wall on a storming ladder and found himself alone except for three followers, one with the sacred shield. He was shot through the breast, but finally rescued by his army. This was the last of many wounds which he received during his expeditions, so that he could rightly say: "There is no part of my body, in front at any rate, remaining free from wounds" (Arrian, *Anabasis.* VI, 10). His impetuosity and passion for glory were such that he could not keep aloof from danger.

Before reaching the Indus Delta, Krateros was sent westward through Arachosia to Carmania with the wounded and other soldiers no longer fit for military service. When he reached Patala, a city of the Brahmans at the beginning of the Indus Delta, he thought he had arrived at the southernmost edge of the inhabited world; for the Indian Sea he believed to be the ocean stream surrounding the earth. At the mouth of the Indus he built a harbor and docks. Sailing out into the Indian sea he offered sacrifices to Poseidon and flung his golden libation cup into the sea, praying that the sea might bring Nearchos and his fleet safely home.

While Nearchos made his voyage through the Indian Sea to the Persian Gulf, Alexander himself marched with the army, through Gedrosia, in order to support the fleet by digging wells and forming depots of provisions on the coast. But his guides lost their way and for sixty days they all suffered from lack of water and food in the Gedrosian desert, Alexander sharing the hardships of his men, declining water when there was not enough for all. He finally reached Carmania, where he rejoined Krateros. The fleet landed after eighty days and the reunited army enjoyed feasts and athletic sports. In 324, with the army and the fleet, he returned to Susa, as the lord of Asia and the then known world of the Far East.

In Susa, Alexander settled the disorders which had broken out during his long absence. He put to death several faithless Persian satraps for governing badly, installed others, and reorganized his whole empire. The Macedonians were still the leading military power and the Greeks the leading cultural element; but Alexander strove more and more to weld together his Asiatic and European subjects into a great Macedonian-Persian universal Empire. He strove for a true unity between Macedonians and Persians. He broke with the classical Greek conception, that all non-Greeks were barbarians. He believed that harmony, peace, and fellowship could reign among all men without regard to their race. He tried to attain this goal by a mass marriage at the victory feast in Susa for the conquest of the Persian Empire. Alexander himself married Barsina, a daughter of Darius, Hephaestion married her sister, and eighty officers married daughters of the Persian aristocracy; ten thousand of his soldiers married native women. Thirty thousand native youths who had received Macedonian training were now enrolled in the army.

This attempt to unite the Persians and the Macedonians into one world and to fuse the races and customs brought a revolt on the part of the Macedonians stationed at Opis on the Tigris. They were reconciled, and a banquet for nine thousand persons sealed the reconciliation. Alexander, however, sent ten thousand veterans back under Krateros who was to become regent of Macedonia, and asked the former regent Antipater to bring him new troops.

Not only the Macedonians, but also the Greeks of the mainland were by now discontent with the behavior of Alexander. He ordered the cities in 324 B.C. to take their political exiles back, which were numerous. As he had not the right to interfere with the internal affairs of the cities he requested that he be recognized by the Greeks as a god. This gave him the same unlimited authority in the Greek cities which he had in Egypt as the son of Ammon and in Persia as the Great King. It thus was a political not a religious measure. The cities of the League of Corinth granted him the honor, and it was probably at this time that the Corinthians set up a statue of Alexander as Zeus (Pausanias, V, 25, 1). This may have been used for the Neison gem (fig. 25).

While the power of Alexander grew, he lost more and more friends. His best friend Hephaestion, the only one who had fully understood him, died in 324 at Ecbatana. When Alexander returned to Babylon in 323, he honored

Hephaestion as a hero, providing a royal pyre and a luxurious funeral. He was full of plans for an Empire embracing Macedonians, Greeks, and non-Greeks, particularly the Persians, into a perfect fusion and harmony. He planned, by circumnavigating Arabia, to establish sea routes between India, Persia, and Egypt. He was now a recognized Empire ruler to whom ambassadors of the Greeks and of foreign people came with petitions on innumerable questions. But in 323, at the height of his glory, after a stormy reign of less than thirteen years, he died of fever. He had led a short life full of valor, and he left behind immortal glory. His last plans, the circumnavigation of Arabia and the exploration of the sea route between Mesopotamia and Egypt, the exploration of the Caspian Sea, the irrigation of Babylonia, and the draining of Lake Copais in Boiotia, could no more be carried through. They show his restless mind, his insatiable ambition to acquire fresh territory, to use new harbors, to colonize the seaboards and islands and to connect by sea all parts of his Empire, which he wanted to bind together as a political and cultural whole. These plans show indeed a genius at work, but his body was worn out too early. His ideas, however, lived on through the Hellenistic

The conception of his personality in the different periods is best reflected in his portraits.

It is very likely that the influence of Apelles and Pyrgoteles grew when Alexander began to aspire to the rule of a great unified Empire. This role called for his portrayal as a super-human, divine personality, whereas Lysippos had always represented Alexander only as a supreme human conqueror. Lysippos seems to have received fewer assignments from Alexander at this period than before, for he was free to accept a commission of
and Roman times, and were by and by realized.
Krateros for a memorial of a celebrated lion hunt, in

which Krateros had come to the rescue of the king in deadly combat with a lion (Plutarch, *Alexander* 40, 4). His collaborator in this group was Leochares, who must have been an old man at that time and probably also less in favor with Alexander than he had been with Philip. Leochares' part in the work was probably small, for Pliny (34, 64) names only Lysippos as the artist. There are only unreliable and weak copies of this work.[29]

Nor does any copy exist of any of the portraits of Alexander by Apelles either of his Alexander in a triumphal chariot, which later was on the forum of Augustus at Rome (Pliny, 35, 93-95), or of his Alexander on horseback at Ephesus, where the horse was so realistic that a real horse is said to have neighed at it (Aelian, *Var. Hist.* II 3). Yet a good idea may be gained of his art, his technique in four colors (white, yellow, red, black, and their mixtures, but no blue), his ethos, and particularly his conception of Alexander, from the mosaic copy of the battle of Alexander with Darius (*Alexandri proelium cum Dario,* Pliny, XXXV, 10) by Philoxenos of

[29] Longpérier, A. de, in *Revue numismatique,* nouv. série *13*: 309, 1908, considers a medallion from Tarsus a copy of this work. See note 87. Loeschcke, G., in *Arch. Jahrb.* 3: 190, pl. 7, 1881, publishes a bad relief from Messene as a copy of the group. *Cp.* refutation of this identification by Bernoulli, J. J., *op. cit.,* 152-153, and Fuhrmann, H., *Philoxenos von Eretria,* 243-244, 246-249. Room for the group and inscriptions: Courby, F., *Fouilles de Delphes* II: 237-240, figs. 187-191. Poulsen, F., *Delphi,* 291-292. Perdrizet, P., in *Jour. Hell. Stud. 19*: 273-279, pl. XI, 1899, considers a Hellenistic gem; *Fuhrmann, H., op. cit.,* 228-270 describes a mosaic in Palermo, fig. 9, pls. VIII-IX, and a sigillata goblet of M. Perennius, 245-247, fig. 10 as reflections of the group.

[30] Ujfalvy, C. de, *op. cit.,* pl. XVIII. Schreiber, Th., *op. cit.,* 73, fig. 11. Winter, F., *Das Alexandermosaik aus Pompeii,* Strassburg, Schlesier & Schweikhardt, 1909. Bernoulli, J. J., *op. cit.,* 31-32, fig. 4. Fuhrmann, H., *Philoxenos von Eretria,* Göttingen, W. F. Kaestner, 1931. Rostovtzeff, M., *Social and Economic History of the Hellenistic World,* I: 128, pl. XVII, Oxford, Clarendon Press, 1941. Pernice, E., Pavimente und figürliche Mosaiken, in *Die Hellenistische Kunst in Pompeji* VI: 90, 1938.

Eretria (figs. 28-29).[30] The painting was commissioned by Cassander, who became ruler of Macedonia in 317/6. It was probably done in Athens, brought to Macedonia and then taken to Rome with the booty of the battle of Pydna, 168 B.C., in which Aemilius Paullus defeated Perseus. Here it was copied, about 100 B.C., for the owner of the Casa del Fauno. It is probably a monument not of one battle, but of a combination of the heroic deeds of Alexander on the Granicus in 334, when he was in great personal danger, at Issos in 333, and at Gaugamela in 331, when he led his army in person against Darius, who had to abandon his chariot and flee for his life.

In this picture Alexander is still without a diadem. He is shown with straight, wild and dishevelled hair fluttering in the wind as a consequence of the rapid movement. His eyes are wide open in rage and violent emotion, and the eyebrows are contracted. The face is unduly lengthened, with long cheeks and chin. He has full lips. There is a sparse beard at the sides and the face in general is unshaven. Thus with the features drawn out of their normal form, the portrait cannot be used for determining Alexander's permanent characteristics. Yet it is a character portrait, showing the emotion and mood of the mighty conqueror under the tension of the moment. In the portraits by Apelles the king certainly was shown in far more ceremonious and serene majesty. But in this battle picture the details of the rich corselet, the weapons, and the harness of the horse Bucephalus, are so realistically depicted that it must be assumed they were based on the originals which could be studied in Athens or in Macedonia. In several points the style agrees with that reported for works by Apelles. The right hand of Alexander with the lance, and the right hand of the charioteer with the whip stand out of the surface as did the hand of Apelles'

Alexander in Ephesus. The horse Bucephalus is so full of life and vigor that the story of how a real horse neighed at him in Ephesus might well have been told of this one too. Pliny (35, 88) says that the likeness in Apelles' portraits was so revealing as to be almost indiscreet. The same thing might be said of the ugly features of Alexander on the mosaic. It is in agreement with Alexander's later politics that Darius is treated by the artist with the same high esteem as Alexander. The Persian king is not thinking of himself but turns back to the friends who lay down their lives in order to enable him to escape.

Reflections of the art of Pyrgoteles, aside from gems, may be found in the first place on coins issued by Alexander, which in this period begin to lend the features of Alexander to the head of the young Herakles (fig. 30). This was the traditional obverse type of the Macedonian coins because the Macedonian kings traced their descent back to the Heraclid Temenos (Isocrates, *Philippus,* 109ff). Alexander, therefore, as before him Philip, in his lifetime kept the head of Herakles on the obverse of his coins (fig. 30). After his death this heroic head was assimilated to the features of Alexander (figs. 31-33). It has been shown convincingly how the head of the ancestral hero was by and by remodelled to take the features of Alexander.[31]. It seems to me that particu-

[31] Seltman, Ch., *Greek coins,* 212: "the head of Heracles has frequently the features of Alexander himself." Hill, G. F., *Historical Greek coins,* 103, pl. VII, no. 59: "Head of young Herakles r., with features resembling Alexander's." Gebauer, K., in *Athen. Mitt. 63/4*: 2-18, pls. 1-3, 1938/39. List of the articles of Newell, E. T., on the coinage of Alexander, in *ibid.,* 2, note 2. *Cp.* also Schreiber, Th., *op. cit.,* 164-67. Neuffer, E., *op. cit.,* 47-48. Seltman, Ch., *Greek coins,* 207-215, pls. XLVIII-XLIX. For coins minted in Babylon see Gebauer, K., *op. cit.,* 14-15. Our fig. 39 is taken from his pl. 3, fig. 17. The coins were minted 331-319 B.C. On coins with Alexander assimilated to Herakles, see Tondriau, J., in *Revue de Philologie, de Littérature et d'Histoire anc.,* sér 3, 23: 47-48, 1949. For the coins issued at Pella (fig. 30) see Newell, *Alexander Hoards II,* Demanhur, 1905. The American Numismatic Society, Notes and Monograms. New York, 1923, pp. 71ff., pl. III.

larly the coins of Sicyon, Sidon and Babylon (figs. 31-33) were meant to be idealized portraits of Alexander. The portraits on the coins were certainly not inventions of the different mints and certainly could not have been made from study of the king himself. They must have been dependent on works of art; of these, gems would have been much more convenient models for the profile views on the coins than sculpture in the round. The same is true of the coins of the following period. The conception of Alexander first as the descendant of Herakles and then himself as Herakles, or as son of Zeus Ammon and later as Zeus himself was probably much furthered by the two counrt artists Apelles and Pyrgoteles. These conceptions were much more in agreement with the taste of Alexander in his later years and with that of his successors, the diadochi, then the sober and intellectual conception of Lysippos. The achievements and designs of colossal dimensions in this period display a genius at work. It cannot be wondered at that Alexander not only believed himself under divine protection, and a descendant of Herakles, but in moments of exaltation he may have believed in, and boasted of divine origin. He is said by a late writer to have dressed occasionally as Ammon, Artemis, Hermes, or Herakles with lion's skin and club (Ephippos in Athenaeus XII, 537 e.f.). Nevertheless, he probably did not himself introduce his effigy on his coins, but allowed the head of Herakles to be made in his likeness. He did not have temples or altars in his lifetime. The swelling of the forehead, the fiery look and the excited tension which characterized the great conqueror are well rendered in the coins.

IV. THE PERIOD OF THE DIADOCHI (323-300)

Alexander's body was embalmed after his death, and taken first to Damascus, then by Ptolemy to Memphis, and at last to Alexandria. Here he reposed in a mausoleum in the center of the city at the intersection of two main streets. He left only one child, a son, by Roxane, born about the time of his death; but this boy, later named Alexander IV, was killed in 311 on the order of Cassander, the son of Antipater.

Alexander's life story crystallized more and more into a romance, and his deification progressed rapidly. In 324 he had demanded and received official deification from the Greek cities. This was not necessary in Egypt, where as a Pharaoh he was a god like his Egyptian predecessors. The priests of Ammon-Re had already proclaimed him as a son of this god in 332.[32] The successors of Alexander, who built their own power on the feats of the great conqueror, and the artists employed by them stressed more and more the divine character of the man.

Thus Abdalonymos, the king of Sidon, who owed his scepter to Alexander, represented him on the sarcophagus, which he ordered during his lifetime according to Oriental custom, with the lion skin helmet and with handsome, elegant features, in accordance with the Herakles coins of Alexander (figs. 30-32). These coins were issued probably during his last years or (like fig. 33) before October 320 and certainly then were in-

[32] For the deification of Alexander: Neuffer, E., *op. cit.,* 11-21, 39-53. Robinson, C. S., Alexander's Deification, in *Amer. Jour. Philol.,* 64: 286-301, 1943. Tarn, W. W., *Alexander the Great,* II: 347-374, 1948. Tondriau, J., *op. cit.,* 41-52, 1949.

terpreted as representing Alexander. The elongated cheeks, the protruding forehead, straight nose with slightly hanging tip, the full lips and the short, rounded chin are the same on the coins and the sarcophagus (figs. 34-36). This is usually known as the Alexander sarcophagus and is now in Constantinople (Istanbul).[33] It represents battles between Greeks and Persians and hunting scenes. The large and radiant eyes of Alexander on the sarcophagus are similar to those of the Alexander Rondanini (figs. 6-8). Though the arrangement of the left part of the battle scene is similar to that of the mosaic (fig. 28) the mood is absolutely different. The features are calm with the exception of the eyes, to which the well-preserved color gives special life, a liquid gaze and a charming expression, but without great emotion. The head of Alexander in the lion hunt (fig. 35), represented on the other long side of the sarcophagus, is conceived in a still more idealized and typical maner than the one in the battle scenes (figs. 34 & 36). It is to be noted that in both reliefs not Alexander but another person occupies the center of the stage. In the battle scene the central figure is probably Hephaestion, who had died before Alexander, and corresponding to Alexander at the right is an old general, perhaps Parmenio. In the lion hunt Abdalonymos himself dominates the

[33] Hamdy Bey and Théodore Reinach, *Une Nécropole royale à Sidon,* pls. 25-30, Paris, Leroux, 1892. Winter, F., *Der Alexandersarkophag aus Sidon,* Strassburg, Trübner, 1912. Ujfalvy, C., de, *op. cit.,* pl. I, fig. 1. Bernoulli, J. J., *op. cit.,* 118-122, fig. 40. The connection with Abdalonymus and the coins first recognized by Studniczka, F., in *Arch. Jahrb.* 9: 204, 226-227, 241-244, 1894; *idem,* Kunst an Kriegergräbern, in *Neue Jahrb.,* 309, 1915. For the coins of Tarsus *cp.* Newell, E. T., Tarsos under Alexander, in *Amer. Jour. Num.* 52: 69-115, pls. I-VIII, 1918. Gebauer, K., *op. cit.,* 8-10, pls. 1-2, nos. 6-10; for those of Sidon, *ibid.,* 10-13, pls. 2-3, nos. 11-16. Our figs. 31-32 are in the Newell collection, American Numismatic Society, New York. Fig. 33 is dated before October 320 B.C. I owe the photographs and information to Agnes B. Brett.

scene in the center, while Alexander seems to be coming to his aid against the lion.

Two marble heads of Alexander in Athens, one found in the excavations on the Ilissos, now in the Acropolis Museum, the other found below the Acropolis, now in the National Museum, wear the lion skin of Herakles to indicate the descent of Alexander from this hero (figs. 37-38).[34] They agree with the coins minted in Sicyon, Sidon and Babylon (figs. 31-33).

A head with lion helmet, found in Sparta, now in the Museum of Fine Arts at Boston (fig. 39a-b), has been identified by Professor Erik Sjöqvist of Princeton University as a portrait of the young Alexander perhaps created by Lysippos.[34b]

While this idealized and calm conception was probably derived from portraits made in the lifetime of Alexander, his immediate successors, the diadochi, turned to new conceptions and probably new artists for the now deified Alexander. The earliest coins minted from the beginning with the intention of presenting a real portrait of Alexander are those issued by Ptolemy I as satrap from about 318 B.C. (figs. 40-42).[35] They heap divine symbols on

[34] Oikonomides, Al. N. in *Archeion Pontou,* 22 (1958), pp. 234-243; *Idem,* in *Athene,* XXII (1961), pp. 26, 29, Figs. 6 and 6a; Papaspyridi, S. in *Guide* to the Athens National Museum, p. 86, No. 366.

[34b] E. Sjöqvist, "Alexander Herakles, a Preliminary Note," in *Bulletin of the Museum of Fine Arts* 51, 1953, pp. 30-33, figs. 1, 4, 5; Oikonomides, *Athene, loc. cit.,* fig. 7. Arndt, *Porträts,* pl. 486. *Greek, Etruscan and Roman Art.* The Classical Collection of the Museum of Fine Arts, Boston, 1963, p. 144, fig. 146.

[35] These first coins with the deified Alexander minted in Alexandria are dated by Svoronos, J., *Münzen der Ptolemäer* III; pl. I 12-23; IV: 7-9, in 317-311 B.C. Gebauer, K., however, *op. cit.,* 14, 18-19, following Regling, K., dates already from 323. The tetradrachms in Boston, figs. 40-41, are dated about 318 B.C. Fig. 42 is from a coin belonging to the Berlin Museum. Lange, K., *Herrscherköpfe,* 42-43. Head, Barclay V., *Historia Numorum,* 848-849, figs. 373-374. Cahn, Herbert A., *Frühhellenistische Münzkunst* (Promotionsrede Basel, 1945), 13-14, figs. 10-11.

Alexander: the ram's horns of Ammon, the elephant's scalp of Dionysus, the aegis of Zeus. The elephant skin reminds at the same time of his victories in India. The diadem is laid like the fillet of Dionysus over the forehead. The features show fully developed Hellenistic style. But, although the lower part of the forehead is bulging, the eyebrows are drawn with an exaggerated angle, the nose is formed with a harsh break above its tip, the cheeks are strongly modelled, and the mouth is separated from them with sharp horizontal lines; yet the main individual features are the same as on the contemporary portraits: the large eyes, the elongated cheeks, the full lips, the tip of the nose, extended somewhat downwards, and the short rounded chin. The model for the coin portrait may have been the cult statue which Ptolemy erected at Alexandria in connection with the state cult for the founder of the city. Lysippos, whose Alexander with the spear probably stood in Alexandria, cannot have been the artist of the cult statue, and his work not the model of the coin, for he had refused to acknowledge or express the divine nature now attributed to Alexander, believing that Alexander's ingenious nature was enough to make him ruler of the earth. Furthermore, it can be assumed from the portrait of Seleucus in Lysippean style, that Lysippos continued to make realistic, not heroized portraits.[36]

The second conception of the deified Alexander is found on the coinage of Lysimachus of Thrace, beginning about 297 B.C. (figs. 43-46).[37] The only divine symbol

[36] See Johnson, Franklin P., *Lysippos,* 230-231, pl. 49. Arndt-Bruckmann, *Porträts,* pls. 101-102.

[37] Gebauer, K., *op. cit.,* 20-22. Bernoulli, J. J., *op. cit.,* 27-28, pl. VIII, 4. Hill, G. F., *Historical Greek coins,* 121-124. Imhoof-Blumer, 14, pls. I, 1; II, 1-3. Cahn, Herbert A., *op. cit.,* 20, fig. 19. Regling, K., *Die antiken Münzen,* 59-60, Berlin, 1929. *Cp.* the excellent evaluation of the coins of Lysimachus by Hinks, R., *Greek and Roman portrait sculpture, British Museum,* 9-10 to fig. 2b, 1935: "The coin-portraits of Alexander are less reliable as an iconographic

here is the ram's horn of Ammon. The diadem is laid in the usual way, its ends and the full locks of hair fluttering in a most lively movement. The features are similar to those on the Alexandrian coins of Ptolemy I (figs. 40-42) but they are still stronger and the eyes are still larger to emphasize the marvelous intelligence of the great conqueror and Great King of Asia. This may reflect the influence of the gems of Pyrgoteles.

The excellence of these portraits indicates that in this period really great portrait statues of the deified Alexander must have existed, for in all times the Greek portraitist represented the whole figure, and not merely the head. On the reverse of some early gold staters of Ptolemy I, Alexander stands on a chariot drawn by elephants, clad in the aegis and holding a thunderbolt. In sculpture we have for this period only one statuette which, however, does give something of the greatness of the subject. The

guide than might have been expected. They are untouchable originals, it is true, but none are contemporary. The earliest and best is the noble head on the tetradrachms of Lysimachus, issued about twenty years after Alexander's death; yet this represents not the man but the divinized son of Ammon, as is shown by the ram's horns in the hair. It has been suggested that this beautiful head was borrowed from the gem by Pyrgoteles: certainly a great artist was responsible for it. Only the pose of the head, however, the expressive glance from the deep-set eye, and the mane of hair are the authentic marks of the Alexander types, and these general traits rather look back to the earlier conception of the Greek portrait as an ideal reconstruction, than suggest that Alexander's own effigies made an immediate contribution to Hellenistic portraiture."

For good enlarged illustrations of the Alexander coin portraits: Hill, G. F., *L'Art dans les Monnaies grecques,* 40, pl. IX, 1, 2, 4. Ujfalvy, C. de, *op. cit.,* 12, fig. 2; 122, fig. 36; 165, fig. 75. Lange, K., *Herrscherköpfe des Altertums,* 40-45, 1938. *Cp.* Head, Barclay V., *Historia Numorum* (284-285, fig. 170. Our fig. 44 is in the Boston Museum, also used by Robinson, Ch. A., *Alexander the Great,* frontispiece. Our fig. 43 is in Berlin, Lange. K., *op. cit.,* 42-43. Our fig. 45 is minted for Lysimachus in Magnesia on the Maeander, and fig. 46 at Lampsacus in Mysia. These two coins are in the Newell Collection of the Amer. Numismatic Society. I owe the photographs to the kindness of A. B. Brett.

statuette, found in Priene (figs. 47-49),[38] is only one-third life-size, and only the upper part is preserved. But its high quality reflects the greatness of larger statues. It shows a strongly built man with the aspect and the muscles of an athlete. The left hand, found separately, probably held a sword. The hair is only sketchily executed, but it shows the "lion's mane" with the ends falling over the forehead. The features are similar to those on the coins issued by Lysimachos at Magnesia on the Maeander (fig. 45). They are also similar to later Ptolemaic coins, which are simpler than the earlier coinage. The nose of the Priene statue is too straight for accuracy. The eyes are deeply shadowed and the mouth is finely modelled. The statuette was found in a house of the third century, dedicated to the cult of Alexander, and may have been made around 300 or even soon after his death, for Priene had to be grateful to him for the funds he provided for the building of the large temple of Athena.

[38] Kekulé von Stradonitz, R., *Sitzungsberichte der Berliner Akad.*, 280-288, 1899. Wiegand-Schrader, *Priene,* 180-182, *figs.* 176-177. Bernoulli, J. J., *op. cit.,* 58-61, fig. 15. Ujfalvy, C. de, *op, cit.,* pls. XII-XIII. Gebauer, K., *op. cit.,* 53-54, K 44. Suhr, E. G., *op. cit.,* 96-98, fig. 12.

V. THE ALEXANDRIAN CONCEPTION OF ALEXANDER (THIRD AND SECOND CENTURIES B.C.)

Ptolemy I, Alexander's earliest and most intimate friend and one of his most skillful generals, became satrap of Egypt after the death of Alexander and king in 306; but he dated his reign from the death of Alexander, for whom he instituted an official state cult in the capital of Alexandria. He founded many Macedonian and Greek colonies in Egypt. Nevertheless, he won the confidence of the Egyptian inhabitants by his clever treatment and regard for their usages, monuments, and religious institutions. He made his capital, Alexandria, a center of art and industry and furthered science, philosophy, and literature. He founded the celebrated Museum, dedicated to the Muses, the largest library at that time. Thus art also flourished under him and his immediate successors.

At the magnificent tomb of Alexander in the royal quarter of the city of Alexandria a cult of the deified conqueror developed. Gradually Alexander became a god himself and was put on a level with Zeus. Just as in other Hellenistic sanctuaries small statuettes of the gods who were venerated there, were dedicated, particularly in sacred precincts of Asklepios and Aphrodite, so also in Alexandria many small and cheap figures of Alexander in soft limestone, with marble or limestone heads and stucco hair, were made and dedicated to him.[39] The first cameos carved with his portrait also seem to have been cut in Alexandria.[40] The two best and largest ones of those preserved, now in Leningrad (fig. 3) [41] and in Vienna (fig. 4),[42] were probably made there in the third century B.C. On these, as on the coins of Ptolemy, several attributes of gods were bestowed on Alexander, to lend more dignity to his appearance. On the cameo in Leningrad he is shown with a helmet crowned with laurel and wearing the aegis. On the Vienna cameo his helmet is decorated with a snake, the thunderbolt, and the head of Ammon. The profile in both cases resembles that on the coins of Ptolemy but the expression is much softer and the modelling less vigorous. The head of the woman next to that of Alexander has been rightly interpreted as that of Olympias. On the cameo in Leningrad she is crowned with laurel, on that in Vienna, with a diadem decorated with an Egyptian lotos ornament and a veil. Her features resemble those on late contorniates of Macedonia and the medallion of Abukir (fig. 2). It was Olympias who had started the belief in Alexander's divine origin by her tale of the snake which had visited her. This probably was one of the reasons why she was

[39] Schreiber, Th., *op. cit.,* 41-56, figs. 6-8, pls. I.B.—III and IV, H. Bernoulli, J. J., *op. cit.,* 34-39, figs. 5-8. Watzinger, C., in *Expédition Sieglin* Vol. II, Part 1B: 1-7, nos. 1-3, figs. 1-2, pls. I-VI, 1927. Gebauer, K., *op. cit.,* 33-51, pls. 6-14. Arndt, P., *op. cit.,* pls. 921 and 926. Graindor, P., *Bustes et Statues-Portraits d'Égypte Romaine,* 73, pl. XXII, 1.

[40] Furtwängler, A., *Die antiken Gemmen* III: 155-156.

[41] Furtwängler, A., *op. cit.,* I, pl. LIII, 2; II, 251-252. Bernoulli, J. J., *op. cit.,* 126-130, pl. IX, 1. Maximova, M. I., *Cameo Gonzaga,* 1924.

[42] Furtwängler, A., *op. cit.,* I: pl. LIII, 1; II: 250-251; III: 151-152. Bernoulli, J. J., *op. cit.,* 130-131, pl. VIII, 1. Eichler-Kries, *Die Kameen im Kunsthistorischen Museum, Wien,* 47-48, no. 3, pl. I, 1927. Modern: neck and end of helm crest. Eichler interprets these portraits wrongly as Ptolemy II and Arsinoe II.

allowed to share divine honors in Alexandria with her son.

Of the small heads of the third century from Alexandria, perhaps the best is the one now in Stuttgart (figs. 50-52).[43] It is similar to that of the cameos, but still softer in the peculiar Alexandrian manner, which is a development of the Praxitelean school. All transitions have been glossed over and vigor has given place to languor and delicate sentiment. The beauty of Alexander is stressed, and the melting look in his eyes noted by Plutarch. The masculine and leonine aspect, however, has disappeared, just as in the later Ptolemaic coins. A coin from Lampsacus in Mysia (fig. 46) dated 291/90 is similar in style for the face, but the hair is similar to the other Lysimachos coins (figs. 43-45).[44]

The largest and artistically best of the heads found in Alexandria is the one probably of the second century B.C. in the British Museum (fig. 53).[45] It has the bend of the neck, the melting look of the upturned eyes, a thick mass of curled hair, which, however, lacks the arrangement of upraised hair of a lion's mane, and instead hangs rather long over the forehead. Its authenticity as a head of Alexander has been doubted, but it does probably represent the great conqueror divinized, with his

[43] Schreiber, Th., *op. cit.,* 45-52, pl. II, C. Bernoulli, J. J., *op. cit.,* 37-39, figs. 7-8. Watzinger, C., *op. cit.,* II: 1-2, pls. I-III. Suhr, E. G., *op. cit.,* 100-101, fig. 14.

[44] For the Ptolemaic coins see Svoronos, J., *Die Münzen der Ptolemäer* III: pl. I, 12-24; IV: 7-9. Our fig. 46 is a coin from Lampsacus in the Newell Collection of the American Numismatic Society. I owe the photograph to the late Agnes B. Brett.

[45] Schreiber, Th., *op. cit.,* 45-46, 51-52, pl. II, D. Bernoulli, J. J., *op. cit.,* 62-65, pl. VI. Ujfalvy, C. de, *op. cit.,* pl. XIV. Hinks, R., *op. cit.,* 9, pl. 9, *British Museum Catalogue of Sculpture* III, no. 1857. Suhr, E. G., *op. cit.,* 98-100, fig. 13. Gebauer, K., *op. cit.,* 38-39, K 9; he discusses this under his earlier group, though dating it later. Laurenzi, L., *Ritratti Greci,* 126, pl. XXXIV, no. 86, Florence, Casa Editrice Sansoni, 1941.

outward appearance idealized to suit the conception of deification. That Alexander's real features have been modified and become blurred is also obvious from the fact that the bending of the neck and the turning of the face are in directions opposite to those attested by literature and by copies of contemporary portraits.

Another large head from Alexandria, now in Cleveland (figs. 54-55),[46] shows similar beautiful features, but they are marked by an even greater softness. The liquid glance of the eyes is still present, and the mouth is opened with an expression of yearning. The cheeks and the parts around the mouth are subtly modelled. The richly curled hair has traces of red, which indicates that it was probably painted reddish blond. The back and sides of the head were modelled in stucco after the Alexandrian fashion. This technique has contributed still further to the softness and tenderness of surface execution.

A fine Hellenistic head, also found in Alexandria, is now in Copenhagen (fig. 56).[46b] It combines Lysippean features with the more subtle modelling of the Hellenistic era.

Another idealized portrait of Alexander from the island of Cos, now in Constantinople (Istanbul, figs. 57-58),[47] about one-third more than life-size, seems to represent Alexander as saviour. This head was found on a terrace dedicated first to Apollo and later to

[46] Gebauer, K., in Arndt, *op. cit.*, pls. 1201-1202; *idem*, in *Athen. Mitt.* 63/64: 44, K 23, 1938/9. He dates it in the second century B.C. Bieber, M., *Art in America*, 121 and 124, fig. 13, 1943.

[46b] F. Poulsen, *Catalogue* no. 441. *Billedtavler* XXXII. Vagn Poulsen, *Les Portraits grecs*, p. 58f., no. 31, pl. XXIII. Arndt-Bruckmann, *Porträts*, pls. 471-472.

[47] Bieber, M., in *Arch. Jahrb.* 40: 167-182, pls. 6-8, 1925. Gebauer, K., in *Athen. Mitt.* 63/64: 58-59, K 48, 1938/9. He dates it at the end of the second century. Tondriau, J., in *Revue de Philologie* 23: 48, 1949, wrongly quotes me as having named this head Alexander as Herakles.

Asklepios. With it were found fragments of a statue to which it belonged, now lost. It was probably the one beheld in the second century by Nikander, as reported by Karystios of Pergamon (in Athenaeus XV, p. 684 E), who saw the ambrosia plant, a symbol of immortality, growing on the head of the figure. Such a plant might well have taken root in the eyeopening of the now lost helmet (*cp.* reconstruction in figs. 59-60).[48] This helmet must have enhanced the effective framing of the face by the sharply twisted long curls of the hair. The complicated movement of neck and head is much emphasized. The features are in simple and large planes, but richly modelled in detail. Thus there is a deep hollow between the rounded chin and the full lower lip. The upper lip is beautifully curved. The well preserved nose is broad and straight, and sharply divided from the cheeks. The eyes are noble in character, with deep corners, and the transition to the cheeks is delicately handled. They are large, wide open, and gazing upward with an expression of deep feeling. The forehead protrudes over the eyebrows. The forms here are more solid than those in the heads from Alexandria and more in the tradition of the youthful portraits of Alexander, though not so close to the latter in spirit as is the almost contemporary head in the Musée Guimet (fig. 11).[49]

All these heads show that the tradition of idealization was prevalent during the third century and still partly in the second century. This tradition is also noticeable on coins, for example on the coins of the island of Cos, particularly one now in Berlin, with the name of the magistrate Klymenos,[50] which shows the lion's scalp on the head. Another coin from Cos, in Berlin, has the

[48] Reconstruction by Bruno Schröder. *Cp.* Bieber, M., *Op. cit.,* 172-173, figs. 5-6.

[49] See note 18.

[50] Bieber, M., *op. cit.,* 178, fig. 10b.

head wearing the lion's skin in three-quarter view (fig. 61) and it agrees with a portrait of a gold ring in the Metropolitan Museum (fig. 62) in such a remarkable way that some connection between the two must be assumed.[51] On the coins of Cos the youthful Herakles takes the place of the bearded Herakles, and there is no doubt that—as on the late coins issued by Alexander —Herakles was interpreted as showing the features of Alexander. The same is true on a coin in Boston, dated 250-200 (fig. 63), and a similar one in Giessen, in the possession of Gertrud Küster (fig. 64).

The head of a bronze statuette in the British Museum (figs. 65-67),[52] is similar to the head from the Asklepeion on the island of Cos, in the attitude of the neck and head, in the thick wavy hair and, it seems, in the Corinthian helmet. A similar head may be seen on an emblem found in the excavations at Begram (fig. 68), now in the Musée Guimet.[53] The features, however, seem to me too insignificant for a representation of Alexander.

[51] I owe the photograph of the coin to Professor Rudolph Herzog; of the gold ring to Dr. Gisela Richter. Mus. No. 10, 132, 1. See Richter, G.M.A., *Catalogue of Engraved Gems, Greek, Etruscan and Roman. The Metropolitan Museum of Art,* New York. 22 F., no. 81, pl. XIV. Similar coins from Cos, *British Museum Catalogue of Greek Coins, Caria and Islands,* 200-204, pl. XXXI, 13-19, dated *ca.* 190-166? Regling, K., *Die Münze als Kunstwerke,* 137, no. 864, pl. LII, dates *ca.* 200 B.C.

[52] Walters, H. B., *Catalogue of the Bronzes in the British Museum,* Pl. 24, Fig. 3; Oikonomides, Al. N. in *Athene,* XXII (1961), pp. 28-30, Figs. 13-15.

[53] The head from Begram with helmet (fig. 68), Kurz, *Begram,* p. 129f., nos. 97-98, figs. 299-437. It has been explained as an Ares by Moebius, "Alexandria und Röm," *Abh. Bayr. Akademie d. Wiss.* 59, 1964, pp. 20ff., pl. III, 5-6. On the other hand Moebius following Curtius explains the many later Macedonian and Roman coins and cameos with the ruler seen from the back, wearing aegis and holding a lance, as inspired by a lost Alexandrian portrait of Alexander (Curtius, *Museum Helveticum* 8, 1951, pp. 215-222; Moebius, *op. cit.,* p. 21f., pl. IV).

The statuette may represent a Ptolemy or another diadoch who imitated Alexander.

In the later coins of the Ptolemies the heads of Alexander tend to lose their portrait character, just as the coins of the later Ptolemies with the head of the first Ptolemy became conventional repetitions of the older coins. The same is true for the Alexandrian marble heads of Alexander, which tend to lose their portrait character.[53a] Some of these may have belonged to statuettes of Alexander with the aegis of Zeus as defensive armor (figs. 69-70).[53b] They probably have been rightly explained as private dedications by Macedonian soldiers to Alexander. The characteristic features of the great conqueror, however, have been lost in these insignificant gifts of unartistic donors.

[53a] This becomes obvious in the case of the head from Rossie Priory (figs. 102-104) which has been considered to be a doubtful portrait of Alexander as Apollo.

[53b] Perdrizet, P., in *Monuments et Mémoires, Piot 21*: 59-72, figs. 1-7, pls. IV-V, 1913. Schreiber, Th., *op. cit.*, 138-139, 142-145, pl. XII. Gebauer, K., *op. cit.*, 77-78, 104-105, K77.

VI. THE ASIATIC CONCEPTION OF ALEXANDER (SECOND CENTURY B.C.)

The fate of the different Greek states—and with it their art—changed during the second century B.C. in some to the worse, in others to the better. The influence of the growing power of Rome made itself felt everywhere. Egypt under the later Ptolemies, who were much weaker than their predecessors, had to accept the Roman senate as guardian. The Romans interfered also in Asiatic politics. After they had defeated Antiochus III in the battle of Magnesia in 190 B.C., Syria was struck from the list of great powers. On the other hand, the able Attalids, who sided with the Romans, increased their territory and might. Bactria gained supremacy in central Asia and even ruled for a while in the Punjab in India, which had once been invaded by Alexander. The rulers of all these states continued to consider Alexander as their ideal model and forerunner.

Therefore, while the Alexandrian school decayed, the Asiatic school of sculpture flourished in the second century, particularly under the Attalids at Pergamon. The head of Alexander which was found there and is now in Constantinople (Istanbul) (figs. 71-72)[54] may be assigned to the period of the great altar built by Eumenes

[54] Winter, F., *Altertümer von Pergamon* VII, 1: *Skulpturen,* 147-149, no. 131, Beiblatt 21, pl. XXXIII. Bernoulli, J. J., *op. cit.,* 80-82, figs. 23-24. Hekler, A., *Bildniskunst,* pl. 59. Ujfalvy, C. de, *op. cit.,* 174-178, pl. XXII, figs. 77, 81-82. Bieber, M., *op. cit.,* 180-181, fig. 11. Gebauer, K., *op. cit.,* 56-57, K 47. Laurenzi, L., *Ritratti Greci,* 126, pl. XXXIV, no. 87.

II (197-159). This grandiose and impressive head may have been based on a portrait made during the last years of Alexander, when hardship and trial—particularly the campaign in India, the retreat through the desert, the revolt of his army, and the loss of his best friends—had worn out his body, ravaged his features, furrowed his brow prematurely, and laid deep shadows around his eyes. Similar signs of premature aging may be seen today in the faces of young veterans of modern warfare. The cheap expedient of achieving idealization by curling the hair is scorned. Alexander is shown with straight hair as in the Azara herm and the mosaic (figs. 13-17 and 28). The expression is full of pathos and of pothos, that is that passionate and ambitious longing which had driven Alexander farther and farther into the unknown East until he had reached what he believed was Oceanus, the boundary of the inhabited world. The "lion's mane" and the movement of the neck may have been derived from a portrait by Lysippos, but the conception is in the vein of the purely Hellenistic emotion, the so-called baroque.

A similar romantic conception of Alexander as Lord of Asia and the conquerer of India in a rather baroque style may also be seen in coins of the first half of the second century, thus in the coins of Priene minted about 200-190 (fig. 73), in those of Miletus, minted about 190-170 (fig. 74), in those of Agathocles of Bactria, who was king of northwestern India about 170-150 (fig. 75), and the rare coin of Mesembria in Thrace, inscribed with the signature of the artist ANT on the lion's scalp above the paw, minted about 150 B.C. (fig. 76).[55] The same

[55] The coins, figs. 73-74 from Priene and Miletus are in the Newell Collection, American Numismatic Society. *Cp.* for coins of Priene with Alexander: Regling, K., *Die Münzen von Priene,* 37-44, pl. II, 32-39; III, 40-43, Berlin, Schöltz, 1927. Coin of Agathokles of Bactria: Gardner, Percy, ed. R. S. Poole, *British Museum Cata-*

conception and the same baroque spirit was later taken over by the Romans, who considered themselves rightly heirs to the empire of Alexander. Even as late as the third century of the Christian era a head of the Pergamon type was used on a gold medallion of Abukir (fig. 114, see below).

The statue to which the head of Pergamon originally belonged may have been a Hellenistic adaptation of a statue by Lysippos. A bronze statuette in Grado near Aquileia (fig. 77) seems to be a Roman copy of such a Hellenistic emotional remodeling.[56] As in the Louvre statuette (fig. 18) it held a spear in the left hand, had its head turned and raised and the feet in a walking position. But the attitude has much more swing and passion than the Louvre statuette. The head is turned much more and lifted to the left instead of the right. The body has a strong bow-like curve. In addition to the spear in the left hand a sword with scabbard is carried in the right hand, and a small chlamys is wound around shoulders and left upper arm. From this statuette it is possible to gain an idea of the essential character of a second-century statue of Alexander.

A late second-century statue of Alexander from Magnesia, now in Constantinople (figs. 78-79),[57] has the

logue of Indian Coins, Greek and Scythic Kings of Bactria and India, XXVIII-XXIX and 10, pl. IV, 1, 1886. *Cambridge Anc. Hist.,* volume of plates II: 10-11, no. c. Schreiber, Th., *op. cit.,* 176-177, fig. 19. Regling, K., *Die ant. Münzen,* 56-57, Berlin, 1929.

Coin of Mesembria in Thrace, in the Ros Collection, Zurich. Lederer, Ph., Ein Beitrag zum Münzbildnisse Alexanders des Grossen, in *Revue Suisse de Numism.* 28: pl. D, Bern, 1941. I owe the photographs of these four coins to the late Agnes B. Brett.

[56] Lorentz, Fr. von, in *Röm, Mitt.* 50: 333-347, pl. 63, 1935. L'Orange, H. P., *op. cit.,* 26, fig. 10.

[57] Hekler, A., *Bildniskunst,* pl. 64. Reinach, Th., in *Monuments et Mémoires Piot* 3: 155-165, pls. 16-18, 1897. Ujfalvy, C. de, *op. cit.,* 97, fig. 28, pl. VII. Bernoulli, J. J., *op. cit.,* 53-58, figs. 12-14. Schede, M., *Meisterwerke zu Constantinopel* II: pl. 19. Gebauer, K.,

same attribute of a sword, which, however, is already found on the Neison gem (fig. 25) and in the statuette from Priene (figs. 47-49). The date for the Magnesia statue is derived from the forms of the letters in the inscription found with the statue, which bears the signature of the artist Menas of Magnesia, and it is corroborated by the powerful and realistically free arrangement of the himation. The body is broad and strong. The full hair was adorned with a bronze wreath. The features are softer than those of the head from Pergamon (figs. 71-72). They are idealized and even less individual than those of the head from Cos (figs. 57-60). The expression of longing in the eyes and mouth has been toned down. It is Alexander conceived as an Apollo.

A small alabaster head and bust found in Egypt, now in the Brooklyn Museum (figs. 80-85),[58] is certainly a representation of Alexander of the second century B.C. It has the incised eyes which occur already in this period in Egypt in precious stones and gems. The expression is very intense, the gaze of the large eyes is directed upward, the mouth is slightly open. The full wavy hair arranged on the forehead like the mane of a lion, as well as the attitude of the neck and head, agree with other portraits of Alexander. Seven holes, ca. 2 cm. wide, appearing at regular intervals just behind the locks which frame the face probably indicate a wreath bound by a heavy wool taenia, the ends of which hang down over the shoulders from the

op. cit., 59-60, K 49. Laurenzi, L., *op. cit.*, 125-126, pls. XXXIII-XXXIV, no. 85. Mercer, Charles, *Alexander the Great*, New York, 1962, fig. on p. 103.

[58] Brooklyn Museum Egyptian Collection No. 54.162. *Forty Years of Egyptian Collecting*, Brooklyn Museum, New York, 1956, p. 41f, No. 23. I owe to Larissa B. Warren the kind permission to use her notes and photographs assembled by her for a term paper in the Department of Fine Arts and Archaeology at Columbia University. See also: Schefold, Karl, *Meisterwerke griechische Kunst*, Basel 1960, pp. 100 and 272 ff., Fig. VII, 369; Mercer, Charles, *Alexander the Great*, New York 1962, Fig. p. 21.

back. One end appears on the right shoulder; the other must have been indicated on the lost drapery.

The torso which consists only of the upper right arm and part of the breast is broken off in a diagonal line going from below the right breast up to the left shoulder. The missing part must have been of different material. It was probably wrapped in a himation draped from the left shoulder over the back to the upper right arm, crossing the breast from the right hip up to the left shoulder and arm. It is an akrolith which uses, instead of marble, Egyptian alabaster, and is certainly an Alexandrian work.

Another Hellenistic bust of Alexander said to have been found in Macedonia is now in the Stathatos Collection in Athens.[59]

Also to an idealized likeness of Alexander of the late second century may possibly be ascribed a fragment found in Delos, now in the Louvre, the so-called Inopus (fig. 86).[60] It may, on the other hand, be one of the many creations conceived under the influence of the heroized and deified portraits of Alexander. Its date must be around 100 B.C.

[59] *La Collection Hélène Stathatos,* Vol. III, 1963, p. 113, no. 64 bis, Fig. 48 bis.

[60] Bernoulli, J. J., *op. cit.,* 88-89, fig. 27. Michon, Etienne, *Bull. corr. Hell.* 35: 288-301, pl. 10, 1911. Gebauer, K., *op. cit.,* 46, K 28. Dickins, G., *Hellenistic Sculpture,* 26, fig. 20. Suhr, E. G., *op. cit.,* 110-111, fig. 19. Jean Charbonneaux tried to identify the sculptor of this portrait with the artist of the Venus de Milo, and to recognize it as a portrait of Mithridates VI, Eupator. But the so-called "Inopus" resembles neither the Venus de Milo nor the coin-portraits of Mithridates. See Charbonneaux, J. in *Revue des arts* 1 (1951), 8-16. *idem, La Vénus de Milo* (Opus Nobile, No. 6), 1958.

VII. LATE HELLENISTIC AND ROMAN REPUBLICAN CONCEPTION (FIRST CENTURY B.C.)

The growing power of the Romans was challenged for the last time in the first century B.C. by Mithridates VI, Eupator, of Pontus, the last great male Hellenistic ruler. He had in 100-99 conquered Paphlagonia and Bithynia, but the mighty Roman senate forced him to give up the two states. This made him a most dangerous enemy of Rome. With the help of his son-in-law Tigranes of Armenia he again conquered Bithynia and also Cappadocia. The exiled kings asked the Romans for help and this led to the three so-called Mithridatic wars (88-84, 83-81 and 74-64 B.C.). Mithridates had travelled all through Asia Minor and knew that the Greek cities there suffered under the harsh Roman rule. He came to them—as once Alexander had done—as a liberator. With their help he conquered the whole of Roman Asia, and killed not only all Roman prisoners, but had about 80,000 citizens murdered. The Greeks honored him with many statues, and he minted silver tetradrachms with his portrait. These coins and some portraits identified on the basis of these coins show an energetic and passionate expression. Coins minted in Odessus imitate the coins of Lysimachus (see figs. 43-46) only the features of Alexander are replaced by those of Mithridates. On these coins and in a head in the Louvre as well as in a statuette in Pergamon[61] he is represented with the headdress of a lion skin, the anastole, rising of the hair over the forehead, the romantically floating hair and the exalted expression of some of the Alexander portraits. The lion skin was taken by Alexander as a symbol of his descent from Herakles. Now Mithridates considered himself, like Herakles, a benefactor of mankind, engaged in liberating it from evil. There is no doubt that he felt himself a genuine heir and even a kind of reincarnation of Alexander.[62]

It is interesting to note that Pompey, the Roman general who in 66 B.C. won the final victory over Mithridates, not only like his enemy and like Alexander received the surname the Great, Pompeius Magnus, but also like Mithridates tried to imitate Alexander the Great. He wore his hair in the anastole, he furrowed his brow and he looked up like Alexander (Plutarch, *Pomp.* 2. Veilleius Paterculus 2, 29). This attempt of imitating Alexander looks rather ridiculous in the sober and ugly Roman features, as we know them from his coins and from his best sculptured portrait in Copenhagen.[63] Pompey's imitation of Alexander is, however, characteristic for the fact that the Roman conquerors were conquered by the conquered

[61] For the coins of Mithridates see Wroth, W., *British Museum catalogue of coins, Pontus,* pls. VIII-IX. Seltman, Ch., *Greek coins,* 237-238. Hill, G. F., *Historical Greek coins,* 160-163. Newell, E. T., *Royal Greek portrait coins,* 40-42, figs. 3-4. For the portrait in the Louvre: Winter, F., *Arch. Jahrb.* 9: 245-250, pl. 8, 1894. For the group with Mithridates as Herakles liberating Prometheus, see Krahmer, G., in *Arch. Jahrb.* 40: 183-205, figs. 1-2, 11-12, 1925.

[62] See Bieber, M., *The Sculpture of the Hellenistic Age,* 2nd ed. 1961, figs. 480-487. Oikonomides, Al. N., in *Archeion Pontou,* 22 (1958), 234-243. For the statuette in the British Museum: Oikonomides, Al. N., in *Archaeology,* 15 (1962), 13-15.

[63] For the coins of Pompey see Bernoulli, J. J., *Römische Ikonographie* I: 107-111, Münztafel II, nos. 36-48, 51-52. Vessberg, Olaf, *Studien zur Kunstgeschichte der römischen Republik,* 135-137, pl. V. For the head in Copenhagen see *Katalog,* 404-405, no. 597, 1940. Hekler, A., *Bildniskunst,* pl. 155a. Delbrück, R., *Porträts,* XLIII, fig. 17 and XLVI, pl. 32. Arndt, P., *Porträts,* pls. 523-524. Schweitzer, B., *Die Bildniskunst der römischen Republik,* 86-88, figs. 117, 124-125, 1948.

Greeks and adopted all their cultural achievements, adapting them to the Roman character and needs.

Thus, now being masters of all former Greek lands, the Romans continued to erect statues of Alexander in their cities as in the Hellenistic cities. The quaestors of Alexander's homeland Macedonia, Aesillas (93-92) and Quintus Brutius Sura (92-88), substituted for the head of Herakles an idealized head of Alexander characterized by thick, long, and exaggerated curled hair, which stands up on the forehead and cascades down over the ears and the side of the nape of the neck (fig. 87).[64]

The sculptured heads in this and the following period tend toward the colossal in size, with enhancement of the features and of the emotional expression. A good example from the East is the limestone head found by the Swedish Cyprus Expedition in Soli (figs. 88-89)[65] and from the West the marble head in the Capitoline Museum in Rome (figs. 90-91).[66] Both show the anastole and the lion's mane—that is, the hair raised over the

[64] Schreiber, Th., *op. cit.,* 179-180, pl. XIII, 18-19. Head, Barclay V., ed. R. S. Poole, *British Mus. cat. of coins, Macedonia,* 19-20. Hill, G. F., *Historical Greek coins,* 158-160, pl. XII, 92-93. Head, Barclay V., *Historia Numorum,* 240-241, fig. 153. Gaebler, H., *Die antiken Münzen Nordgriechenlands* I, Makedonia und Paionia, Vol. III, 1: 69-73, pl. III, nos. 1-5; Vol. III 2: 9, pl. III, 13-15. Ujfalvy, C. de,*op. cit.,* 157, fig. 70. Gebauer, K., *op. cit.,* 22-23. Our fig. 87 is a coin in the Newell Collection, American Numismatic Society of New York. I owe the photograph to the kindness of Agnes B. Brett. See also the coin minted by Aesillas on title page to plates, collection Bieber.

[65] Gjerstadt, E., in *The Swedish Cyprus Expedition 1927-1931* III: 506; 526-527, no. 520. pl. CLXIII, 1-2, 1937. Westholm, A., The Temples of Soli, in *The Swedish Cyprus Expedition* III: 132, no. 520, pl. XIV, 1936.

[66] Arndt, P., *op. cit., pls.* 186-187. Hekler, A., *Bildniskunst,* pl. 62a. Ujfalvy, C. de, *op. cit.,* pl. III. Schreiber, Th., *op. cit.,* 68-78, pl. V, K. Helbig, W., *Mon. ant. dei Lincei* VI: 73-88,, pl. II, 1895. Bernoulli, J. J., *op. cit.,* 65-69, pl. VII; Stuart Jones, *Sculptures of the Museo Capitolino,* 341-342, Stanza del Gladiatore, no. 3, pl. 85. Laurenzi, L., *op. cit.,* 105-106, pl. XV, no. 41. Restored: pieces of hair on the back of the neck; tip of nose; bust.

forehead, then framing the face and falling down in full strands—and the high forehead, large eyes, broad nose, slightly opened mouth, energetic chin, and long cheeks. The neck is strong and, in the well-preserved Capitoline head, bent toward the right shoulder, while the head is bent to the left and noticeably lifted. Thus, in spite of the fact that the usual vigor of the personal expression is replaced by a more general and almost cold and sophisticated spirit, there is no doubt that this is a portrait of Alexander. The contrasted movements of neck and head are exaggerated. The hair forms a thick and irregular frame around the head. Such luxuriant growth of hair was considered to be the seat of strength and power. The features are large and simple, the eyebrows prominent, the eyes deep-set, the lips full and short. The head has been interpreted as Alexander Helios or as the sun-god assimilated to the type of Alexander. The fact that the quality of the head in Rome is better than that of the provincial and rather clumsy one from Soli is in accord with the fact that the best Greek artists were now working in the Roman capital.

For the Romans as for the later Greeks Alexander was a man of superhuman achievements, who like Herakles had become divine on the basis of his own illustrious deeds.

VIII. CONCEPTIONS DURING THE ROMAN EMPIRE (FIRST TO THIRD CENTURY A.D.)

Since the second century B.C. the Romans had absorbed by and by all the Greek states which once had been under the sway of Alexander. T. Quinctius Flamininus had proclaimed the Greek mainland states free and independent from Macedonia in 197 B.C., but in reality they were subordinated to Roman governors and had to pay tribute to Rome. Egypt and Asia had to obey Roman orders since the same period. Then one state after the other became part of a Roman Empire. In 168 Macedonia became dependent on Rome and in 146 a Roman province. The kingdom of Pergamon was bequeathed to the Romans in 133, and Syria and all Asia followed. Finally Egypt, dependent on the Romans since the second century, was made a Roman province in 30 B.C. after the death of Cleopatra, the last great Hellenistic ruler. The Romans adopted Alexander's idea that harmony, peace and brotherhood ought to unite all mankind without regard to their race. The Romans by and by gave Roman citizenship to all the different people who lived in their Empire. Thus the brotherhood of men which Alexander had wished came true in the Roman Empire. The Romans, therefore, considered themselves, with good reasons, heirs to the empire of Alexander. They gave him the title Alexander Magnus. Augustus, called a friend of Alexander by Strabo (XIII, 594), put Alexander's head on his signet ring (Sueton., *Augustus* 50; see our fig. 62). The artists of the imperial period continued to create portraits of the great conqueror whose life became more and more a legend.

Roman art during the Empire was based mostly on Greek art, but it was not a direct continuation of the late Hellenistic style. Periods of Classicism, when Phidias and Praxiteles were the models, as in the time of Augustus, of the Claudians, and of Hadrian, alternated with periods when Hellenistic emotionalism was the ideal, as under the Flavians and the Antonines. A product of the classicistic tendency was the flourishing of schools of copyists, the best being those of the two first centuries, before and after Christ. To this period belong the good copies of the contemporary portraits of Alexander (figs. 5-27).

It was probably during the Flavian period (A.D. 69-96) that a new conception of Alexander based on the irrational and romantic Hellenistic ideal led to such creations as the colossal heads of Alexander in Chatsworth,[67] the face of which is nine inches long, and from Tarsus in Copenhagen, (figs. 92-93)[68] the latter has remains of an Ammon's horn. Both have a crown of curly hair which frames the face and falls in heavy masses onto the nape of the neck. Over the forehead it stands up in the anastole. Some bronze statuettes have a similar head but are too small to be identifiable.[69] The statues of which the colossal heads were a part must have been of similar rather

[67] Furtwängler, A., in *Jour. Hell. Stud. 21*: 212-214, pls. IX-X, 1901. Ujfalvy, C. de, *op. cit.*, 174-175, figs. 78-80. Schreiber, Th., *op. cit.*, 59-64, pl. IV, G. Bernoulli, J. J., *op. cit.*, 52, fig. 11. Gebauer, K., *op. cit.*, 75, K 72.

[68] Poulsen, F., *Billedtavler*, pl. 33, no. 445. *Idem, Katalog*, 1951, 315, no. 445. Poulsen dates it in the time of Hadrian. Poulsen, Vagn, *Les Portraits grecs*, p. 83, no. 57, pls. XLII-XLIII.

[69] Schreiber, Th., *op. cit.*, 124-128, pl. XI, R, 1. Ujfalvy, C. de, *op. cit.*, 121, fig. 35. There are many other bronze statuettes supposedly of Alexander, as in Schreiber, Th., *op. cit.*, 71, 91-93, 124-129, pls. VI, 2; VIII, 2; XI, 2; 285, fig. 35. Wulff, O., *Alexander mit der Lanze, Bronzestatuette der Sammlung Nelidow*, 1898; and the wooden statuette in the Louvre, in Gebauer, K., *op. cit.*, 37-38, K 7, pl. 5—all of which seem to me too sketchy to be of any help in the study of the portrait of Alexander and have, therefore, been left out of this book.

affected attitude. They represented the deified, not the human, Alexander.

The same is true of two statuettes in Paris, which may belong to this period, one standing, in the Louvre, and one seated, in the Cabinet des Médailles, of Alexander with helmet and weapons. The standing figure in marble, which was found in Gabii (fig. 94-95),[70] is poor in workmanship and in a bad state of preservation, but it has the same exaggerated movement of the head with a still stronger upward turn. The corselet beside the left leg indicates that the statuette is that of a general. The right hand probably held the sword, and the left hand only the scabbard. The strong swing of the hip is patterned after Praxitelean statues. The seated figure in bronze from Reims, in the Cabinet des Médailles of the Bibliothèque Nationale (fig. 96),[71] has a still more heightened sentimentality. The lance in the right hand and the sword in the left are probably correct restorations. The broad body is draped with a mantle in the grand manner. The locks are long, full, and irregular as in the Capitoline head (figs. 90-91). The idea of Alexander as godlike, but at the same time a ruler of the world who trusted his own weapons and was thus on a level with Zeus, is behind these Roman creations, and there was a statue of Alexander as Zeus in Olympia (Pausanias, V, 25, 1).

The cool classicism of the Hadrianic age (A.D. 117-

[70] Bernoulli, J. J., *op. cit.,* 83-84, fig. 25. Schreiber, Th., *op. cit.,* 111-113, pl. VII, N. Gebauer, K., *op. cit.,* 79-80, K 82. Suhr, E. G., *op. cit.,* 108-109, fig. 18. Mercer, *op. cit.,* fig. on p. 61. Restored: part of crest, edge of helmet, part of neck, strip in left shoulder, left hand, right arm, right lower leg, part of left lower leg, left foot, upper corner and lowest portion of corselet.

[71] Babelon, E., and A. Blanchet, *Catalogue des Bronzes de la Bibliothèque nationale,* 356, no. 824. Ujfalvy, C. de, *op, cit.,* pl. V. Schreiber, Th., *op. cit.,* 113-114, pl. VIII, O. Bernoulli, J. J., *op. cit.,* 115-117, fig. 39. Babelon, J., *Choix des Bronzes des Collections de Janzé et Opperman,* 17, pl. III, 1929. The throne is modern but the base is ancient.

138) toned down this false emotional approach in art. A good example of this trend is the over-life-size porphyry head in Paris (figs. 97-98).[72] The hair falls in more regular fashion; the movement, though strong, particularly in the neck, is more natural and the modeling of the features shows a tendency toward artificial construction of the single parts of the face. Thus the eyebrows are broken in sharp angles, the lips are separated from their surroundings by exaggeratedly deep curved lines. The sharp divisional lines are then glossed over with high polish. Alexander has now become the object of arbitrary interpretation, artistically as well as ethically.

It is therefore not to be wondered at that the colossal statue found in the Roman Baths at Cyrene (figs. 99-100),[73] has been interpreted as Dioscurus, as Helios, and as Alexander. It seems likely that the statue is one of Alexander and that the horse beside him is an allusion to his steed Bucephalus. The object in his left hand, of which only the lower part is preserved, is probably the lance. Behind it hangs the chlamys, attached to the left shoulder, where it is collected by a large round fibula. The hair is heavier and more wildly arranged than in any of the older portraits. The excessive use of the drill in separating the single strands dates the figure in the early Antonine period. To the same period belongs the sharp contrast between the dark hair with its strong play of light and shade and the highly polished surface of the face. A similar contrast is found in a probably contemporary over-life-sized statue in Wilton House (figs.

[72] Delbrück, R., *Antike Porphyrwerke,* 60-62, fig. 12, pl. 15. Gebauer, K., *op. cit.,* 79, K 81.

[73] Maviglia, Ada, in *Revue Arch.* sér. 5, 3: 169-183, 1916. Ghislanzoni, E., *Notiziario archeologico* II: 105-122, figs. 47-48, 51, 54, pls. V-VI, 1916. Bagnani, G., in *Jour. Hell. Studies 41*: 237-238, pl. XVII, 1, 1921. Hill, Dorothy, in *Art. Bull.,* 157, note 2, 1942. Laurenzi, L., *op. cit.,* 132, pl. XLI, no. 101.

101a-b).[74] Alexander here seems to be conceived as Apollo. Heads perhaps already of the early third century are in Rossie Priory (figs. 102-104),[47a] in the Barracco Collection (figs. 105-106),[75] and a head in Madrid.[76]

The best and perhaps one of the latest sculptured Alexander portraits is the grandiose head from Ptolemais in the Boston Museum (figs. 107-108),[77] which seems to be of the period of Caracalla (A.D. 211-217). Caracalla, like formerly Mithridates and Pompey, not only imitated the appearance of Alexander in his own attitude, dress, and portraits, but also ordered many pictures and statues of Alexander to be set up everywhere in Thrace; and he filled Rome with statues and pictures of Alexander in the Capitoline as well as in other sanctuaries (Herodianus IV, *Antoninus Caracalla* 8, 1). The face of the Boston head is almost ten inches in length. The forms of the features are still those of Alexander idealized to youthful beauty. The expression is that prevailing in a later age when Alexander has become no longer human, but a hero like Achilles or Herakles, or transfigured to a god

[74] Poulsen, F., *Greek and Roman Portraits in English Country Houses,* 37-38, fig. 9.

[74a] Poulsen, F., *op. cit.,* p. 38f, figs. 10-11. See also our note 53a.

[75] Helbig, W., in *Mon. ant. dei Lincei* 6: pl. 3, 1895. Idem, La *Collection Barracco,* 43-45, 62, pls. 57 and 57a. Arndt, P., *op. cit.,* nos. 477-478. Schreiber, Th., *op. cit.,* 67-71, pl. V, J. Suhr, E. G., *op. cit.,* 92-93, fig. 11. Bernoulli, J. J., *op. cit.,* 77-79, figs. 19-20. Laurenzi, L., *op. cit.,* 106, pl. XVI, no. 42. Mercer, *op. cit.,* fig. on p. 144. H.0.28m. No restorations have been made.

[76] Arndt, P., *op. cit.,* pls. 483-484. Bernoulli, J. J., 84-86, fig. 26.

[77] Helbig, W., in *Mon. ant. dei Lincei* 6: 75-88, pl. I, 1895. Bernoulli, J. J., *op. cit.,* 70-74, figs. 16-17. Arndt, P., *op. cit.,* pls. 481-482. Ujfalvy, C. de, *op. cit.,* pl. IV. L'Orange, H. P., *Apotheosis in Ancient Portraiture,* 34-37, fig. 17. He wrongly considers the Boston head a replica of the Capitoline head, figs. 90-91. Caskey, L. D., has not included it in his *Cat. of Greek and Roman Sculpture, Museum of Fine Arts, Boston,* 1925. Bieber, M., in *Amer. Jour. Arch.* 49: 425, figs. 1-2, 1945, has proved the authenticity of the Boston head. H.0.48 m; length of face 0.243 m. No restorations have been made.

like Apollo or Zeus. The oblique neck is combined with an upturned movement and an emotional look up to heaven.

In the later period of Alexander Severus, beginning in 231 of our era, continuing under Gordian III (242-243), and ending under Philippus II Arabs in 249, coins with portraits of Alexander were minted in Beroia, the capital of the Macedonian League.[78] They show at least five different types.[79] Alexander in one group appears with thick hair fluttering almost horizontally and with the anastole (fig. 110).[80] In another group he has the same anastole, but the hair is encircled by a diadem and hangs almost vertically. Often an Ammon's horn is added (fig. 112).[81] A third type has the head covered by a lion's skin (fig. 113).[82] Diadem, anastole, corselet, and shield are found in another group (fig. 114),[83] and a

78 Gaebler, H., in *Ztschr, für Numismatik* 24: 316-338, pls. VI-VII, 1904; 25: 1-38, pls. I-III, 1906. *Idem, Die antiken Münzen Nordgriechenlands* III, *Die antiken Münzen von Makedonia und Paionia* III, 1: 14-25, 94-196, pl. IV, 11-19; III, 2: 12-18, 47-48, pl. IV, 19-23, pl. XI, 25-28. Schreiber, Th., *op. cit.,* 180-184, pl. XIII, 13-14, 20-23.

79 Gaebler, H., in *Ztschr. für Numismatik* 25: 8-12, 1906; *idem, Münzen von Makedonia* III, *1*: 15, adds five variants. *Cp.* Gebauer, K., *op. cit.,* 22-23.

80 Fig. 110 is taken from *Ztschr. für Numismatik* 25: pl. II, 28, 1906. Other examples, *ibid.,* 24: pl. VI, 6, 10-11, pl. VII, 21-22, 26, 30, 32, 1904; 25: pl. I, 11, pl. II, 27, 30, 1906. *Münzen von Makedonia* III, 1: pl. IV, 12-13; III, 2: IV, 20. Bieber, M., *op. cit.,* 428-429, fig. 3.

81 Fig. 112 is taken from *Ztschr. für Numismatik* 25: pl. II, 35, 1906. Other examples, *ibid.,* pl. I, 5, 6, 10, 12-14, 16; pl. II, 23, 33, 34; pl. III, 39, 40, 43. *Münzen von Makedonia* III, 1: pl. IV, 11; III, 2: pl. IV, 19. Bieber, M., *op. cit.,* fig. 4.

82 Fig. 113 is taken from *Ztschr. für Numismatik* 25: pl. III, 38, 1906. Other examples, *ibid.,* 24: pl. VI, 9; pl. VII, 25, 29, 1906; 25: pl. I, 4; pl. II, 26, 36; pl. III, 47, 1906. *Münzen von Makedonia* III, 1: pl. IV, 14; III, 2: pl. XI, 25. Bieber. M., *op. cit.,* fig. 5.

83 Fig. 114 is taken from *Ztschr. für Numismatik* 25: pl. III, 55, 1906. Other examples, *ibid.,* pl. III, 45, 48. *Münzen von Makedonia* III, 1: pl. IV, 18-19; III, 2: pl. IV, 23. Bieber, M., *op. cit.,* fig. 6.

helmet covers the head in still another type (fig. 111).[84]

Whereas the coins with the Ammon's horn and the lion's skin may have been influenced by the older coins of Lysimachos and of Macedonia (see figs. 30-32), they and particularly the three other types as well seem rather to have been influenced by statues which were in existence then, such as the statues in Cyrene (figs. 99-100), Wilton House (figs. 101a-b) and those from which came the colossal heads in the Capitoline Museum (figs. 90-91), in the Barracco Museum (figs. 105-106), the one found at Ptolemais in Boston (figs. 107-108), and the one found at Tarsus in Copenhagen (figs. 92-93). The reverse of the Macedonian coins shows, in addition to Alexander—fighting, hunting or taming Bucephalus—and his mother Olympias (see above), a temple and a table with prizes.[85] These allude to the festivals in honor of the Roman emperors and the deified Alexander, for which these coins or contorniates were issued. There certainly must have been erected in this and other temples cult statues not only of the emperors but also of Alexander. There were, moreover, portraits of Alexander set up in private chapels. Thus Alexander Severus had one in his Lararium together with the best deified emperors (Aelius Lampridius, *Alexander Severus,* XXXI, 5).

From the coins and the late Roman colossal statues we can learn how these portrait statues of Alexander may have looked. They had the strong expressiveness which is a characteristic of late Roman style. Thick and irregular

[84] Fig. 111 is taken from Gaebler, H., *Münzen von Makedonia* III, 2: pl. XI, 28. Other examples, *ibid.,* III, 1: pl. IV, 15-17; III, 2: pl. IV, 21; pl. XI, 27. *Ztschr. für Numismatik* 25: pl. I. 17; pl. III, 56-57, 1906.

[85] Gaebler, H., in *Ztschr. für Numismatik* 25: 27-29, 1906. For the temples see pl. I, 12; pl. 31. Temple and prize table, pl. III, 41, the reverse of our fig. 112.

strands of hair, expressing power, a noticeable lifting of the head, expressing transfiguration, deepset eyes with a look upturned to heaven, giving an emotional expression.[86] This Roman conception is based on the irrational and romantic Hellenistic conception of Alexander, but it adds exaggerated movement and heightened emotion.

The celebrated golden medallions found at Abukir in Egypt, (figs. 2, 114) in the same country as the Boston head (figs. 107-108), and at Tarsus in Cilicia (figs. 1, 115-116) found in the same place as the head in Copenhagen, (figs. 92-93) are of the same period as the late Macedonian coins (figs. 109-113), as testified by the portraits of Caracalla (211-217) and Alexander Severus (222-235) on some of them.[87] They have been dated in the year 242-243 and explained as prize medal-

[86] For the transfigured Alexander see L'Orange, H. P., *Apotheosis in Ancient Portraiture,* 28-38, figs. 12-17, 1947.

[87] See for both groups: Neuffer, E., *op. cit.,* 18-20. Regling, K., *Die antiken Münzen,*[3] 149-150, Berlin, 1929. L'Orange, H. P., *op, cit.,* 20-21, 24, figs. 4-5. Illustrated together also by Svoronos, J. N., in *Journal int. d'archéol. Numism. 10*: pls. VIII-VIV, 1907. For the medallions from Abukir see Dressel, H., *Fünf Goldmedaillons aus dem Funde von Abukir, Abh. preuss. Akad. d. Wiss.,* with pls. I-IV, 1906. Koester, E., Gold Medallions of Abukir, in *Burlington Mag. 11*: 162-163, 1907. Gebauer, K., *op. cit.,* 23-25. *Newell, E.,* in *Amer. Jour. Num. 44*: 128-130, pls. 14-15, 1910. Doubts cast on the authenticity of these Abukir medallions by Dattari, G., *I Venti Medaglioni d'Abusir,* 1908, and others have been refuted by Dressel and others. See, particularly, Newell, E., *op. cit.,* 130: "It seems to be the present judgment of the best critics that the medallions of Abukir are genuine, and of the period claimed for them; as examples of Graeco-Roman art at its best, they constitute one of the most priceless classical treasures found in recent years." Newell later took a skeptical attitude. See Suhr, E. G., *op. cit.,* 184-186. See also Head, Barclay V., *Historia Numorum,* 241-242: "The authenticity of the twenty remarkable gold medallions discovered in Egypt (at Abukir?) in 1902 is still questioned by some leading numismatists, notwithstanding the powerful arguments in their favor advanced by Dressel (*op. cit.*), which no one has as yet been able to refute." *Cp.* also Bieber, M., in *Amer. Jour. Arch. 49*: 429, 1945. For the medallions from Tarsus see Longpérier, A. de, in *Revue numismatique,* Nouv. Sér., *13:* 309-311, pls. X-XII, 1868. Mowat, R., in *ibid.,* Sér. 4, 7:

lions for victories in the Olympian festival celebrated at Beroia in the presence of Gordian III in that year.[88] The many portraits of Alexander and scenes related to his deeds prove that the contests were given in honor of the deified Alexander. I believe, therefore, that these medallions, like the one representing Philip (fig. 1), are based mostly on statues. The medallion from Abukir in front view (fig. 114) reminds one of the head found in Pergamon (figs. 71-72); but the fluttering strands of the hair and ends of the diadem, the exaggerated emotional expression, and the over-crowding of the corselet and shield with symbolic representations betray Roman taste. The medallion from Tarsus with the lion's skin (fig. 115) is a very free adaptation of the older coins, but the horizontally fluttering hair of the medallion with diadem (fig. 116), with its very schematic arrangement, has its nearest parallel in the contemporary coin of Beroia (fig. 109).

Roman portraits of Alexander are mentioned for a still later period. Trebellius Pollio (*Triginta Tyranni*, XIV, 14, 3-6) says that the family of the Marciani, who were adversaries of Gallienus (260-268) in the period of the thirty tyrants, still in the writer's own days, that is the time of Diocletian (284-305), decorated not only their ringstones, but also their silver plates, the embroideries of the tunics, cloaks and fillets as well as ornaments of every kind with portraits of Alexander. "It is said, that those who wear the likeness of Alexander carved in either gold or silver are aided in all that they do" (Trebellius Pollio, *op. cit.*, XIV, 6). At the end of the fourth century St. John Chrysostomos blamed the people of Antioch,

1, pls. I-II, 1903. Schreiber, Th., *op. cit.*, 189-193, pl. XIII, 16. Bernoulli, J. J., *op. cit.*, 29-30, fig. 3. Ujfalvy, Ch. de, *op. cit.*, 17, fig. 3, and 145, figs. 51 and 55. Gaebler, H., *Münzen von Makedonia* III, 1: 192-194.

[88] See Dressel, H., *op. cit.*, 52-63.

because they wore bronze coins of Alexander the Macedon around their necks and ankles. We have, indeed, named portraits of Alexander until the end of antiquity.

To the third century belong the bronze coins of Elagabalus (218-222) issued at Apollonia Mordiaeum in Pisidia (fig. 117) inscribed "Alexander founder of Apollonia";[89] and to the fourth and perhaps fifth centuries, the contorniates (figs. 118-120) from the Newell Collection in the American Numismatic Society.[90] On the reverse of figure 118 and on the obverse of figure 119 is inscribed ALEXANDER MAGNUS MACEDON; on figure 120 the inscription ALEKKANDER MAG testifies that this head with the lion scalp, the bulging forehead, the exceedingly big eyes expressing superior intelligence, the straight nose, the pouting and expressive mouth, with the radiated sun beside it, is meant to be the deified Alexander the Great. Thus the image and the greatness of Alexander were transmitted to the middle ages. Even Islam adopted him as one of its prophets.

One of the early coins but the one brought to the northern-most part of the Roman Empire was found during excavations in London (figs. 121-122). It is now in the London Museum at Kensington Gardens.

[89] Hill, G. F., *British Mus. Cat. of Coins, Lycia, Pamphylia,* 202, no. 1 and 204, nos. 9-10, pl. XXXIII, 1 and 5, 1897.

[90] I owe the photographs of these contorniates, which are in the Newell Collection of the American Numismatic Society, to Agnes B. Brett. See on contorniates: Alföldi, A., *Die Kontorniaten,* Budapest, 1943. Jocelyn Toynbee, *Roman Medallions, Numismatic Studies,* No. 5: American Numismatic Society, New York, (1944) 234-236 and 243.

From the number and diversity of these artistic expressions it can be seen how the unique personality of Alexander gave to the art of portraiture impulses which—after having been created in his own lifetime—carried on through the Hellenistic and Roman periods.

The liberal ideas of Alexander, giving equal rights to everybody, pushed into the background during the Hellenistic period, came to the fore again during the Roman period. Then, after having been neglected during the medieval, Renaissance, and Baroque periods, they came to life again during the American and the French revolutions in the eighteenth century. Since then they have been promoted by always larger groups of responsible personalities in different countries, such as the men in the revolutionary movements of France and Germany in 1848. While, however, these attempts on liberalism were suppressed in Europe—as they had been in the Hellenistic States—these ideas have taken deep roots in the United States of America. They are now promoted by the United Nations Commission on Human Rights.

LIST OF ILLUSTRATIONS AND SOURCES

The figures are in the same chronological sequence as they occur in the text, according to the figure number. For better comparisons, some figures are on plates other than the group to which they belong. Each figure, therefore, is followed by the number of the plate on which it appears.

I.

Fig. 1., pl. I. Philip II. Medallion from Tarsus. *Revue numismatique,* 4th série VII, 1903, pl. III.

Fig. 2., pl. I. Olympias. Medallion from Abukir. Dressel, *Goldmedallions,* pl. II D.

Fig. 3., pl. II. Alexander and Olympias. Cameo in Leningrad. Bernoulli, *Darstellungen Alexanders,* pl. IX,1.

Fig. 4., pl. II. Alexander and Olympias. Cameo in Vienna, Austria. Eichler-Kries, *Die Kameen,* pl. I.

Fig. 5., pl. III. Head of Youthful Alexander. Athens. Deiktes Phot. Archives, Athens.

Figs. 6-7., pl. VI. Head of Alexander Rondanini. Munich. Phots. Bruckman.

Fig. 8., pl. VII. Alexander Rondanini, Munich. Phot. Bruckman.

Fig. 9., pl. IV. 'Eubuleus', found in Eleusis. National Museum, Athens. Phot. German Arch. Institute, Athens.

Figs. 10a-b., pl. V. 'Eubuleus'. Unfinished bust of Alexander. Found during Agora Excavations, S2089. Hesperia 19. No. 4, 1960. pl. 85 c-d.

Fig. 11., pl. VI. Alexander as Crown Prince. Musée Guimet, Paris. Arndt. *Porträts,* pls. 922-923.

Fig. 12., pl. VII. 'Dressel' Head. Dresden. Copy of a Portrait of the Young Alexander by Lysippos. *Athen. Mitt.* 63/64, 1938/39, pl. 15.

II.

Fig. 13., pl. VIII. Azara Herm. Louvre. Copy from Lysippos. Phot. Giraudon.

Fig. 14., pl. VIII. Azara Herm. Louvre. Ujfalvy, *Type physique d'Alexander,* pl. II.

Figs. 15-16., pl. VIII. Azara Herm, Louvre. Arndt, *Porträts,* pls. 181-182.

Fig. 17., pl. IX. Azara Herm, Louvre. Phot. Giraudon.

Fig. 18., pl. X. Bronze Statuette, Louvre. Probably Alexander with the Lance by Lysippos. Phot. Giraudon.

Fig. 19., pl. XI. Bronze Stauette, Naples. Alexander Riding on Bucephalus, probably from Group by Lysippos, representing the Battle on the River Granicus, 334 B.C. Arndt, *Porträts,* pl. 479.

Figs. 20-21., pl. XII. Detail of Fig. 19. Arndt, *Porträts,* pl. 480.

Fig. 22., pl. XII. Decadrachm. Alexander Riding Bucephalus Fights Poros Riding an Elephant at the Battle on the River Hydaspes (Jhelum). Phot. Deiktes Phot. Archives, Athens.

Fig. 23., pl. XIII. Alexander Riding. Bronze found in Begram, Afghanistan. Phot. Musée Guimet, Paris.

Fig. 24, pl. XIV. Alexander Taming Bucephalus. Bronze Statuette. Museo archeologico, Florence. Phot. Deiktes Phot. Archives, Athens.

Fig. 25., pl. XV. Alexander as Zeus, with Eagle, Thunderbolt and Aegis. Neison Gem. Leningrad. Furtwängler, *Gemmen,* pl. 3, no. 11.

Figs. 26-27., pl. XV. Head in Geneva, Switzerland. Phots. Deiktes, Phot. Archives, Athens.

Figs. 28-29., pl. XVI. Alexander and Darius in Battle of Issus, 333 B.C. Details from Mosaic found in Casa del Fauno. After Painting by Philoxenos of Eretria, related to the Style of Apelles. Museum Naples.

III.

Fig. 30., pl. XVII. Tetradrachms issued in Pella by Philip and Alexander. Found with the Demanhur Hoard in India. Newell, *Alexander Hoards* II, *Demanhur 1905,* the American Numismatic Society, *Notes and Monographs,* New York, 1923, pp. 71ff., pl. III.

Fig. 31., pl. XVII. Tetradrachm, minted in Sicyon, 330 B.C. Phot. American Numismatic Society (ANS).

Fig. 32., pl. XVII. Coin minted in Sidon. Newell Collection. Phot. ANS.

Fig. 33., pl. XXI. Coin minted in Babylon about 324 B.C. Earliest Portrait of Alexander as Herakles. *Athen. Mitt.* 63/64, 1938/39, pl. 3, no. 17.

IV.

Figs. 34a-b., pl. XVIII. Heads of Alexander in Battle Scenes on the Alexander Sarcophagus. Found in Sidon, made for King Abdalonymus of Sidon. Istanbul. Winter, *Alexander-Sarkophag,* colored pl. 17.

Fig. 35., pl. XVIII. Lion Hunt, Scene from Alexander Sarcophagus. Alexander and Abdalonymus. Phot. Deiktes, Phot. Arch., Athens.

Fig. 36., pl. XIX. Alexander in Battle Scene from Alexander Sarcophagus. Phot., Deiktes Phot. Arch., Athens.

Fig. 37., pl. XX. Head, found below the Acropolis. National Museum, Athens. Sjöqvist, *Bulletin of the Museum of Fine Arts,* Boston, 1953, p. 31, fig. 3.

Fig. 38., pl. XX. Head, found in the Ilissos. Acropolis Museum, Athens. Meliades, *Praktika,* 1953, p. 56.

Figs. 39a-b., pl. XX. Head found in Sparta. Museum of Fine Arts, Boston. Sjöqvist, *op., cit.,* pp. 30-33, figs. 1, 4-5.

Figs. 40-41., pl. XXI. Coins issued by Ptolemy I, Satrap of Egypt beginning 318 B.C. Phots. Museum of Fine Arts, Boston.

Fig. 42., pl. XXII. Coin issued by Ptolemy I. Lange, *Herrscherköpfe,* pl. 41.

Fig. 43, pl. XXII. Coin issued by Lysimachus as King of Thrace (306-281 B.C.). Lange, *op. cit.,* pl. 43.

Fig. 44, pl. VII. Coin issued by Lysimachus. Hellenistic Adaptation of the Rondanini Type. Phot. Museum of Fine Arts, Boston.

Fig. 45, pl. XXIII. Coin issued by Lysimachus, minted in Magnesia on the Maeander, about 300 B.C. Newell Collection. Phot. ANS.

Fig. 46, pl. XXIV. Coin issued by Lysimachus minted at Lampsacus in Mysia, 291-290 B.C. Newell Collection. Phot. ANS.

Figs. 47-49, pl. XXIII. Statuette found in Priene. About 300 B.C. Suhi, *Greek Statesman,* fig. 12.

V.

Figs. 50-52, pl. XXIV. Head found in Alexandria. Third Centurn B.C. *Expedition Sieglin* II, p. 18, pls. I-II.

VI.

Fig. 74, pl. XXXIX. Coin found in Miletus. 190-170 B.C. Newell Collection, Phot. ANS.

Fig. 75, pl. XXXIX. Coin found in Bactria, issued by Agathocles. About 170-168/7 B.C. *British Museum Catalogue of Coins, Bactria,* pl. IV, 1.

Fig. 76, pl. XXXIX. Coin from Mesembria in Thrace, about 150 B.C. *Revue Suisse de Numismatique* 28, 1941, pl. D.

Fig. 77, pl. XXXV. Bronze Statuette, found in Grado. Hellenistic Adaptation of Lysippos' Alexander with the Lance (see fig. 18). *Röm. Mitt.* 50, 1935, pl. 63.

Fig. 78, pl. XL. Statue found in Magnesia. Istanbul. Phot. Museum Istanbul no. 549.

Fig. 79, pl. XL. Head of Statue from Magnesia. Phot. Museum Istanbul no. 319.

Figs. 80-85, pls. XLI-XLII. Head and Bust of Alexander carved in Alabaster. Found in Egypt. Brooklyn Museum. Phots. Brooklyn Museum of Fine Arts.

Fig. 86, pl. XLIII. So-called 'Inopus'. Found in Delos. Louvre. Phot. Musée du Louvre.

VII.

Fig. 87, pl. XL. Coin minted by Aesillas in Macedonia, 93 B.C. Newell Collection. Phot. ANS.

Figs. 88-89, pl. XLIV. Late Hellenistic Head, found in Soli, Cyprus. *Swedish Cyprus Expedition* III, 1937, pl. CLXIII, figs. 1-2.

Figs. 90-91, pl. XLV. Early Roman Head. Capitoline Museum, Rome. Bernoulli, *Darstellungen Alexanders,* pl. VII.

VIII.

Figs. 92-93, pls. XLVI-XLVII. Head found in Tarsus. Copenhagen, Ny Carlsberg Glyptotek. Vagn Poulsen, *Les portraits grecs,* pls. XLII-XLIII.

Fig. 94, pl. XLVIII. Statuette found in Gabii. Flavian Period (A.D. 69-96). Louvre. Bernoulli, *Darstellungen Alexanders,* fig. 25.

Fig. 95, pl. XLVIII. Head of Statuette from Gabii. Deiktes, Phot. Archives, Athens.

Fig. 96, pl. XLIX. Bronze Statuette, Flavian Period. Cabinet des Médailles. Phot. Bibliothèque Nationale, Paris.

Figs. 97-98, pl. L. Porphyry Bust, Hadrianic Period (A.D. 117-138). Louvre. Delbrück, *Porphyrwerke,* pl. 15.

Figs. 99-100, pl. LI. Statue found in Cyrene, North Africa. *Notizario Archeologico* II, 1916, pls. V-VI.

Figs. 101a-b, pls. LII-LIII. Statue of Alexander in Wilton House, England. F. Poulsen, *Portraits in English Country Houses,* pl. 9.

Figs. 102-104, pls. LIV-LV. Head in Rossie Priory, England. F. Poulsen, *op. cit.,* pls. 10-11.

Figs. 105-106, pls. LVI-LVII. Head in Collection Barracco, Rome. Arndt-Bruckman, *Porträts,* pls. 477-478.

Figs. 107-108, pl. LVIII. Head found in Ptolemais, Cyrenaica. Museum of Fine Arts, Boston. Arndt, *op. cit.,* pls. 481-482.

Figs. 109-113, pls. LIX-LX. Alexander on late Macedonian Coins issued about A.D. 231-249. *Zeitschrift für Numismatik* 25, 1906. pl. II.

Fig. 114, pl. XXXVIII. Medallion from Abukir. Alexander in rich Armour. Based on Type of Pergamon figs. 71-72. Dressel, *Goldmedaillons,* pl. II C.

Figs. 115-116, pl. LXI. Alexander on Medallions from Tarsus. *Revue numismatique* 7, 1903, pls. I-II.

Fig. 117, pl. LXII. Coin issued by Elagabalus in Apollonia Mordiaeum, Pisidia. Newell Collection, Phot. ANS.

Figs. 118-120, pl. LXII. Contorniates, Newell Collection. Phot. ANS.

Figs. 121-122, pl. LXIII. Tetradrachm with Alexander as Herakles. Found in excavations at London. Phot. London Museum, Kensington Gardens.

Fig. on title page for plates. Coin minted by the Quaestor Aesillas in Macedonia, 92-88 B.C. Collection Bieber. Phot. ANS. Cf. fig. 87.

PLATES

1. Philip II. Medallion from Tarsus.

2. Olympias. Medallion from Abukir.

3. Alexander and Olympias. Cameo in Leningrad.

4. Alexander and Olympias. Cameo in Vienna, Austria.

PLATE II

5. Head of Youthful Alexander, Athens.

Plate III

9. 'Eubuleus' found in Eleusis.

PLATE IV

10a.

10b.

10a-b. 'Eubuleus,' from Agora Excavations. Agora Museum, Athens.

PLATE V

6-7. Alexander Rondanini, probably by Leochares, about 338 B.C.

11. Alexander as Crown Prince. Musée Guimet, Paris.

Plate VI

44. Coin issued by Lysimachus. Hellenistic Adaptation of Rondanini Type.

8. Alexander Rondanini. Munich.

12. Young Alexander. Dresden, formerly Dressel Collection.

PLATE VII

13.

14.

15.

16.

13-16. Azara Herm, Louvre.

PLATE VIII

17. Azara Herm, Louvre.

Plate IX

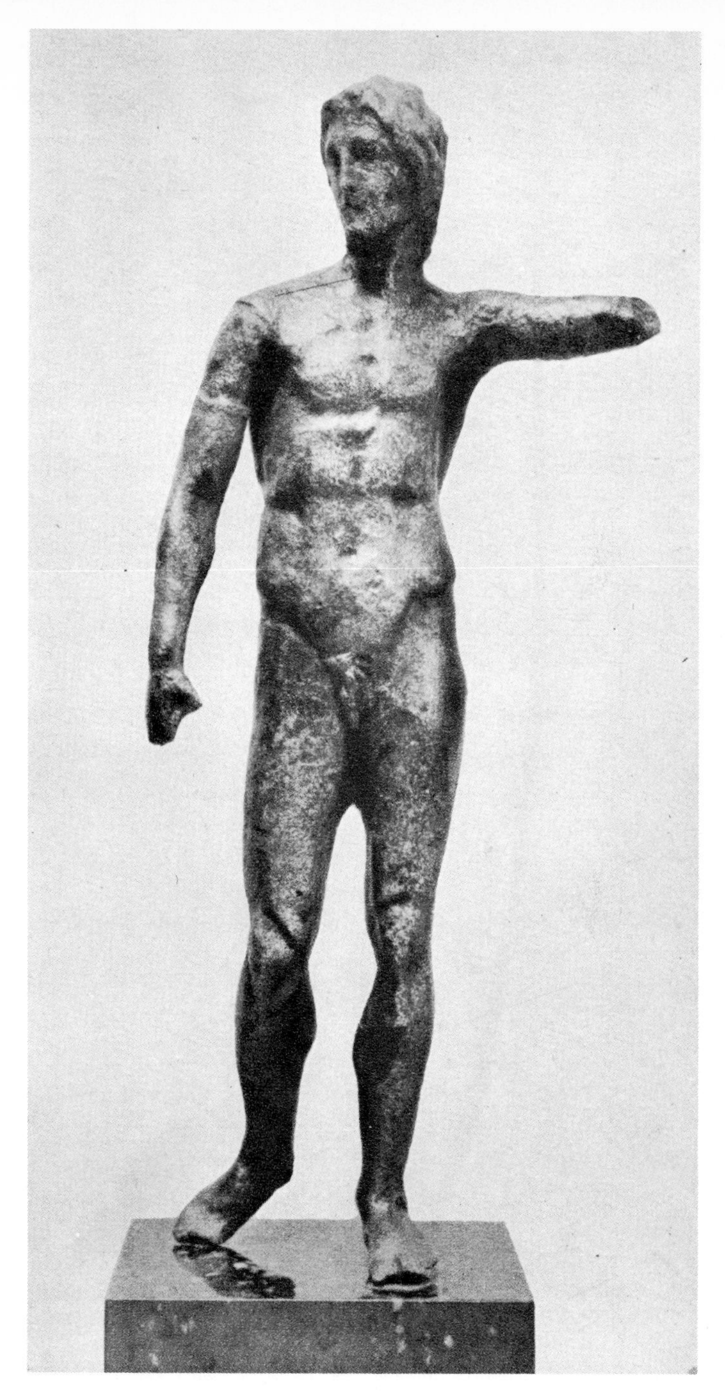

18. Bronze Statuette. After Lysippus, Alexander with the Lance.

PLATE X

19. Alexander on Bucephalus. Probably from Group by Lysippus representing the Battle on the River Granicus, 334 B.C. Naples.

PLATE XI

20. 21.

20-21. Bronze, Naples. Battle on the River Granicus.

22. Alexander on Bucephalus fights Poros on Elephant. Decadrachm, British Museum.

23. Alexander riding. Bronze found in Begram. Musée Guimet, Paris.

PLATE XIII

24. Taming of Bucephalus. Bronze, Museo Archaeologico, Florence.

PLATE XIV

25. Neison Gem. Leningrad. Perhaps after Apelles.

27.

26.

26-27. Head, Geneva, Switzerland.

PLATE XV

28.

29.

28-29. Battle of Alexander and Dareios, after Philoxenos.
Mosaic found in Casa del Fauno. Naples Museum.

Plate XVI

30. Coins issued in Pella by Philip and Alexander.

31. Coin minted in Sicyon about 330 B.C.

32. Coin minted in Sidon.

PLATE XVII

34a.

34b.

34 a-b. Heads of Alexander in Battle Scenes. Alexander Sarcophagus.

35. Lion Hunt. Alexander Sarcophagus from Sidon. Istanbul.

Plate XVIII

36. Alexander in Battle. Alexander Sarcophagus found in Sidon. Istanbu

PLATE XIX

Alexander-Herakles. Athens, National Museum.

38. Alexander Head found in Ilissos. Acropolis Museum, Athens.

39b.

9 a-b. Alexander-Herakles found in Sparta. Boston Museum of Fine Arts.

PLATE XX

33. Coin minted in Babylon.

40. Coin issued by Ptolemy I.

41. Coin issued by Ptolemy I.

PLATE XXI

42. Coin issued by Ptolemy I.

43. Coin issued by Lysimachus.

Plate XXII

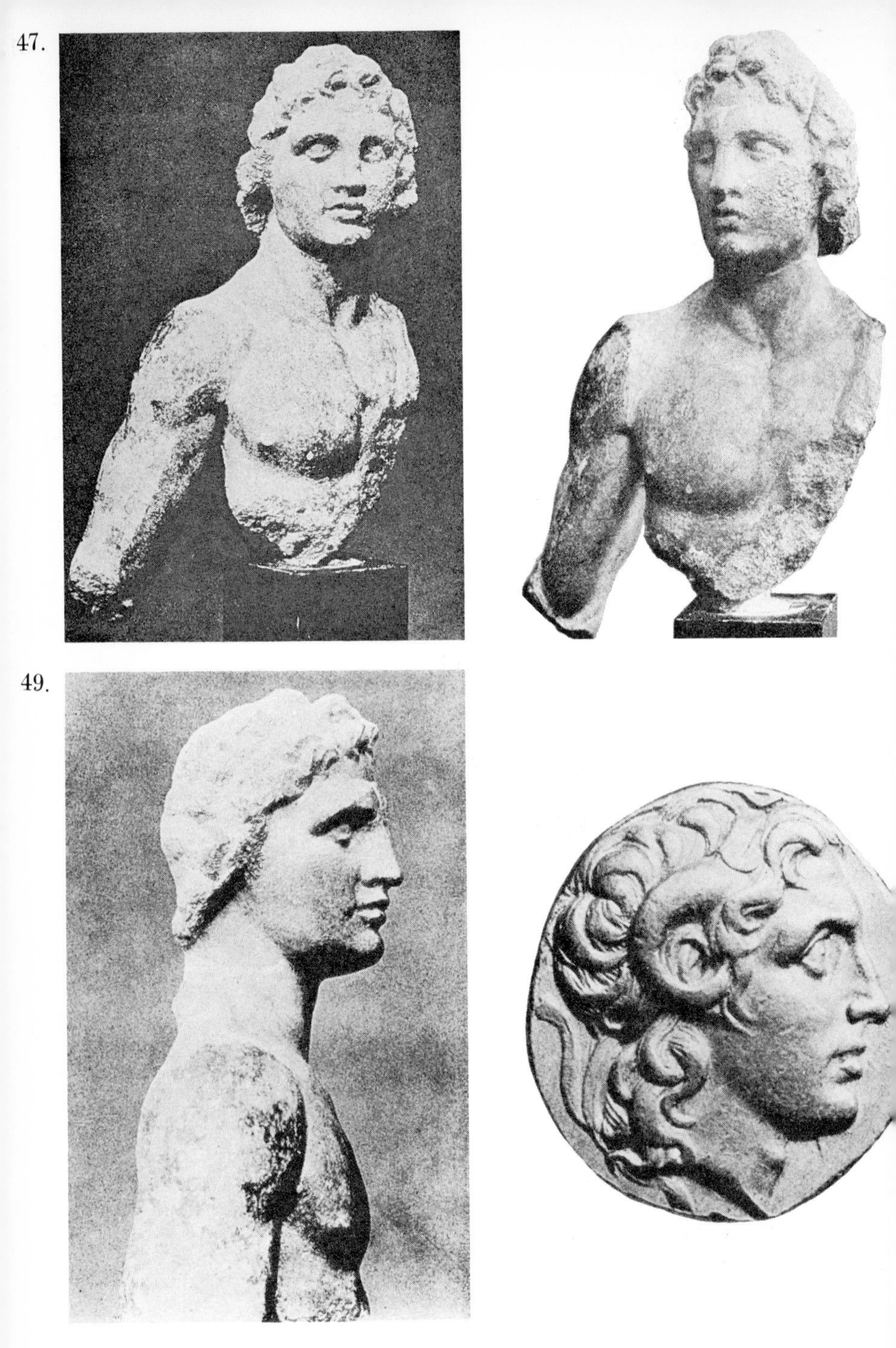

47-49. Statuette found in Priene.

45. Coin minted in Magnesia on Maeander, issued by Lysimachus

PLATE XXIII

0-52. Head found in Egypt. Museum of Stuttgart.

46. Coin minted in Lampsacus, issued by Lysimachus.

PLATE XXIV

53. Head found in Alexandria, Egypt. British Museum.

PLATE XXV

54. Head found in Alexandria, Egypt. Cleveland Museum.

PLATE XXVI

55. Head found in Alexandria, Egypt. Cleveland Museum.

Plate XXVII

56. Head found in Alexandria, Egypt. Ny Carlsberg Glyptotek, Copenhagen.

Plate XXVIII

57.

58.

57-58. Head found in the Sanctuary of Asklepios in Cos. Museum of Istanb

PLATE XXIX

59.

60.

59-60. Reconstruction of Head from Cos.

PLATE XXX

61. Coin found in Cos. Berlin.

62. Gold Ring. Metropolitan Museum of Art, New York.

PLATE XXXI

63. Coin minted about 250-200 B.C. Boston Museum of Fine Arts.

64. Coin in Collection of Gertrud Küster. Giessen, Germany.

PLATE XXXII

65. Bronze. Alexander or Ares. British Museum.

PLATE XXXIII

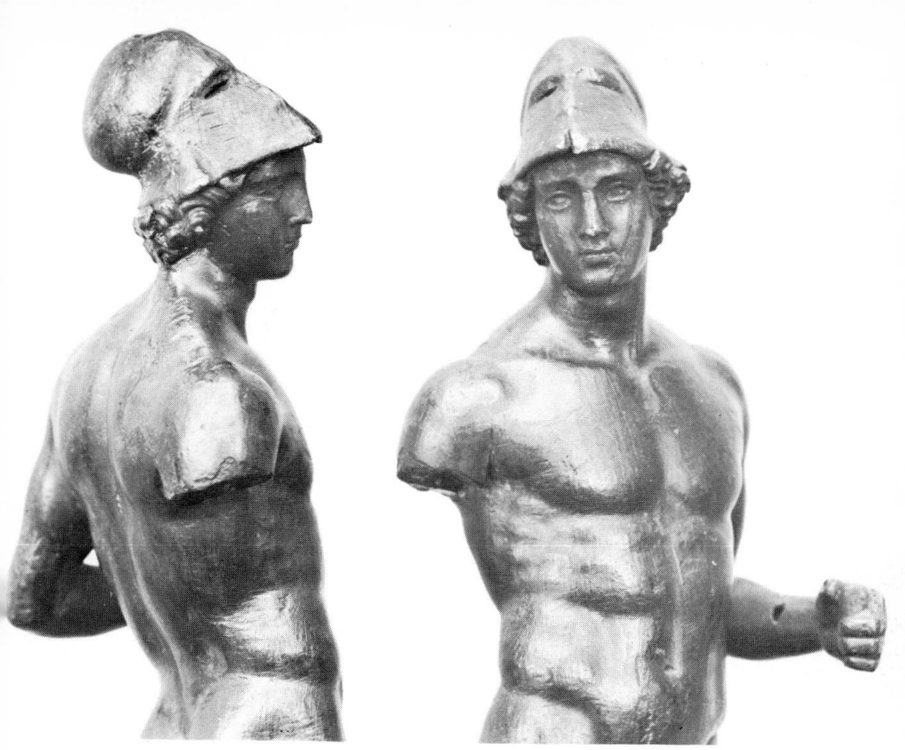

66-67. Front and Profile of upper part of Figure 65.

68. Stucco Emblem found in Begram, Afghanistan. Musée Guimet, Paris.

PLATE XXXIV

69-70. Statuettes of Alexander with large Aegis. 69. In Cairo. 70. In Louvre.

77. Bronze found in Grado near Aquileia, Northern Italy.

PLATE XXXV

71. Head found in Pergamon.

Plate XXXVI

72a. Head found in Pergamon. Profile of Figure 71.

PLATE XXXVII

2b. Three quarter View of Figure 71.

114. Medallion from Abukir. Alexander in Three quarter View.

73. Coin found in Priene, ca. 200-190 B.C.

74. Coin found in Miletus, ca. 190-1 B.C.

75. Coin issued by Agathocles of Bactria, ca. 170 B.C.

76. Coin minted in Mesembria, Thrac ca. 150 B.C.

PLATE XXXIX

79.

78.

78-79. Statue found in Magnesia.

87. Coin minted by Aesillas in Macedonia, 93 B.C.

PLATE XL

80.

82.

80-82. Alabaster Bust found in Egypt
Brooklyn Museum.

81.

PLATE XLI

84.

83.

85. Alabaster Bust found in Egypt.
Brooklyn Museum.

85.

PLATE XLII

86. So-called 'Inopus,' found in Delos. Louvre, Paris.

PLATE XLIII

89.

88.

88-89. Late Hellenistic Head. Soli, Cyprus.

PLATE XLIV

90.

91.

90-91. Early Roman Head. Capitoline Museum, Rome.

PLATE XLV

92. Head found in Tarsus, Asia Minor. Ny Carlsberg Glyptotek, Copenhagen.

Plate XLVI

93. Profile View of Figure 92.

PLATE XLVII

4.

95.

94-95. Statuette found in Gabii. Louvre.

PLATE XLVIII

96. Bronze Statuette. Cabinet des Médailles, in Bibliothèque Nationale, Paris

PLATE XLIX

97.

98.

97-98. Hadrianic Porphyry Bust. Louvre, Paris.

PLATE L

99.

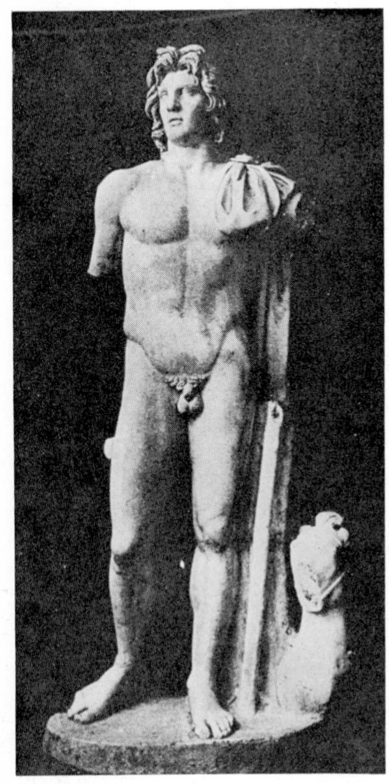

1

99-100. Statue found in Cyrene, North Africa.

PLATE LI

101a. Statue in Wilton House, England.

Plate LII

101b. Head of Statue in Figure 101a.

Plate LIII

102. Roman Head. Rossie Priory, England.

PLATE LIV

103.

104.

103-104. Profile Views of Figure 102.

105. Roman Head. Collection Barracco, Rome.

Plate LVI

106. Profile View of Figure 105.

PLATE LVII

107.

108.

107-108. Head found in Ptolemais, Cyrenaica. Boston Museum of Fine Arts.

109-110. Alexander on Late Macedonian Coins.

PLATE LIX

111-113. Late Macedonian Coins.

PLATE LX

115.

116.

115-116. Alexander on Medallions from Tarsus.

Plate LXI

117. Alexander on Coin issued by Elagabalus in Apollonia Mordiaeum, Pisidia.

118.

119.

120.

118-120. Alexander on Contorniates. Newell Collection. American Numismatic Society, New York.

121.

122.

121-122. Coin with Alexander, Reverse Zeus. Excavated in London. London Museum, Kensington Gardens.

INDEX

INDEX OF MODERN SCHOLARS

(Numbers in parentheses indicate footnotes)

GENERAL INDEX

Key to abbreviations:
A. = Alexander
portr. = portrait
ptg. = painting
st. = statue
stte. = statuette